New
Beginnings

NEW BEGINNINGS

CELEBRATE THE FRESH STARTS OF LIFE.

EVELYN BENCE
COMPILER

FLEMING H. REVELL COMPANY
OLD TAPPAN, NEW JERSEY

Scripture quotations are from the Holy Bible, New
International Version. Copyright © 1973, 1978, 1984
by the International Bible Society. Used by permission
of Zondervan Bible Publishers.

Library of Congress Cataloging-in-Publication Data

New beginnings.

SUMMARY: A book of inspirational quotations
under categories arranged alphabetically, such
as achievement, courage, happiness, nature,
solitude, and wisdom.
  1. Quotations, English. {1. Quotations]
I. Bence, Evelyn.
PN6081.N49   1988   082   87-28501
ISBN 0-8007-1564-0

Copyright © 1988 by Fleming H. Revell Company
Published by the Fleming H. Revell Company
Old Tappan, New Jersey 07675
Printed in the United States of America

ACKNOWLEDGMENTS

———————— ✌ ————————

Acknowledgment is made to the following for permission to reprint copyrighted material:

AVE MARIA PRESS: Excerpt from *In Memoriam* by Henri Nouwen copyright © 1980 by Ave Maria Press. All rights reserved. Used with permission of the publisher.

WILLIAM COLLINS SONS & COMPANY, LIMITED: Excerpts from *Miracles, Mere Christianity, The Problem of Pain,* and *The Weight of Glory* by C. S. Lewis are used by permission.

DODD, MEAD & COMPANY, INC.: Excerpts from *God Calling* by Two Listeners, edited by A. J. Russell, reprinted by permission of Dodd, Mead & Company, Inc.

DOUBLEDAY AND COMPANY, INC.: Excerpts from *Conjectures of a Guilty Bystander* by Thomas Merton. Excerpts from *A Cry for Mercy* by Henri Nouwen. Excerpt from *Turning* by Emilie Griffin. Excerpts from *Soundings* by Chris Aridas. Used by permission.

WM. B. EERDMANS: Excerpt from Margaret Clarkson, *Grace Grows Best in Winter* (Wm. B.

C.S. Lewis and/or C.S. Lewis. Reprinted by permission of Harcourt Brace Jovanovich, Inc.

HARPER & ROW, PUBLISHERS, INC.: Excerpts from *The Meaning of Persons* by Paul Tournier copyright © 1957 by Paul Tournier. Reprinted by permission of Harper & Row, Publishers, Inc. Excerpts from *Learn to Grow Old* by Paul Tournier copyright © by SCM Press Ltd. Reprinted by permission of Harper & Row, Publishers, Inc. Excerpts from *The Person Reborn* by Paul Tournier copyright © by Paul Tournier. Reprinted by permission of Harper & Row, Publishers, Inc. Excerpts from *The Adventure of Living* by Paul Tournier copyright © 1965 by Paul Tournier. Reprinted by permission of Harper & Row, Publishers, Inc. Excerpt from *These Strange Ashes* by Elisabeth Elliot copyright © 1975 by Elisabeth Elliot. Reprinted by permission of Harper & Row, Publishers, Inc. Excerpts from *Celebration of Discipline* by Richard J. Foster copyright © by Richard J. Foster. Reprinted by permission of Harper & Row, Publishers, Inc. Excerpts from *Clinging* by Emilie Griffin copyright © 1984 by Emilie Griffin. Reprinted by permission of Harper & Row, Publishers, Inc. Excerpt from *If This Be Love* by Calvin Miller copyright © 1984 by Calvin Miller. Reprinted by permission of Harper &

by permission of InterVarsity Press, P.O. Box 1400, Downers Grove, IL 60515.

ALFRED A. KNOPF, INC.: Excerpt from Chaim Potok, *In the Beginning,* copyright © 1975. Used by permission of Alfred A. Knopf, Inc.

LITTLE, BROWN & COMPANY, PUBLISHERS: Some poems by Emily Dickinson are from *The Complete Poems of Emily Dickinson,* edited by Thomas H. Johnson, published by Little, Brown & Company, Publishers.

MACMILLAN PUBLISHING COMPANY: Excerpts from *They Stand Together* by Walter Hooper reprinted with permission of MacMillan Publishing Company. Copyright © 1979 by The Estate of C.S. Lewis.

MULTNOMAH PRESS: Excerpts from *Imagination* by Cheryl Forbes copyright © 1986 by Cheryl Forbes. Used by permission. Excerpt from *The Mystery of Marriage* by Mike Mason copyright © 1985 by Mike Mason. Used by permission. Excerpts from *Growing Strong in the Seasons of Life* by Charles Swindoll copyright © 1983 by Charles Swindoll. Used by permission. Excerpts from *Guidance* by Philip Yancey copyright © 1983 by Philip Yancey. Used by permission.

pany. Excerpt from *Self Talk* by David Stoop copyright © 1982 by David Stoop. Excerpt from *Each New Day* by Corrie ten Boom copyright © 1977 by Corrie ten Boom. Excerpts from *Seeds of Greatness* by Denis Waitley copyright © 1983 by Denis E. Waitley, Inc. Excerpt from *The Double Win* by Denis Waitley copyright © 1985 by Denis E. Waitley, Inc. Excerpts from *Why Us?* by Warren Wiersbe copyright © 1984 by Warren W. Wiersbe. Used by permission.

HAROLD SHAW PUBLISHERS: Excerpts from *Walking on Water: Reflections on Faith & Art* by Madeleine L'Engle used by permission of Harold Shaw Publishers, Box 567, Wheaton, IL 60189. Copyright © Crosswicks, 1980.

SIMON & SCHUSTER, INC.: Excerpt from *The Road Less Traveled* copyright © 1978 by M. Scott Peck, M.D. Reprinted by permission of Simon & Schuster, Inc.

DENIS WAITELY: Excerpts from *The Psychology of Winning* used by permission of the author.

KENNETH L. WILSON: Excerpts from *All Things Considered* used by permission of Kenneth L. Wilson.

WORD BOOKS: Excerpt from *Traveling Hopefully*

by Stan Mooneyham copyright © 1984; used by permission of Word Books, Waco, Texas. Excerpt from *You Can Make a Difference* by Tony Campolo copyright © 1984; used by permission of Word Books, Waco, Texas.

ZONDERVAN PUBLISHING HOUSE: Excerpts taken from IN SEASON AND OUT by John Leax. Copyright © 1985 by John R. Leax. Used by permission of Zondervan Publishing House. Excerpt taken from A FEAST OF FAMILIES by Virginia Stem Owens. Copyright © 1983 by The Zondervan Corporation. Used by permission. Excerpts taken from KNOWING THE FACE OF GOD by Tim Stafford. Copyright © 1986 by Tim Stafford. Used by permission of Zondervan Publishing House. Excerpts taken from LOVING GOD by Charles Colson. Copyright © 1983, 1987 by Charles W. Colson. Used by permission of Zondervan Publishing House. Excerpt taken from CHOICES . . . CHANGES by Joni Eareckson Tada. Copyright © 1986 by Joni Eareckson Tada. Used by permission of Zondervan Publishing House.

CONTENTS

—— ❧ ——

FOREWORD

And so each venture is a new beginning. . . .
                                        T.S. Eliot

A new beginning. A fresh start. A clean slate. There is something almost irresistible about a new beginning. Whether it's starting a new job, moving into a new home, enrolling in a new school, or beginning a new relationship, a new venture makes you feel like a child on the first day of school. Armed with a fistful of newly sharpened pencils and an unsoiled notebook tucked under your arm, you stand prepared for the new adventure. Your stomach flutters with anticipation as you face new challenges and new lessons. Lessons of courage and valor, perhaps. Certainly lessons of achievement and failure.

But above all else, a new beginning represents hope. The January-first sort of hope that you feel when you hang up a brand-new calendar. You sense that you have been given an extraordinary gift: the opportunity to set new goals and to renew your commitment to reaching those goals. And sometimes, you're even given a chance to mend the past.

And so it has been from the first beginning. This unique blend of adventure and hope propels us through life. And during those times when we lose sight of our goals and need encouragement, we look to those who have faced these things before us. Their wisdom—and their humor—is gathered herein to challenge, to refresh, and to offer encouragement.

So begin. And may your journey be filled with many discoveries.

NEW BEGINNINGS

Some people remain Scouts all their lives. They take pleasure in wearing the juvenile uniform complete with its mysterious decorations. It is not difficult to see that they also retain an infantile personality; in some way they have become fixed at a stage of youthful adventure. They have not accepted the law of adventure, which is that it must die in order to be born again. It is in fact through the continual dying of even our most exciting adventures that we reach maturity. In this way we are made available for other adventures, adventures which will be less infantile and naive, more adult and fruitful.

PAUL TOURNIER

The Adventure of Living

'Tis well an old age is out,
And time to begin a new.

JOHN DRYDEN

Things are always at their best in their beginning.

BLAISE PASCAL

❧

It was the best of times, it was the worst of times.

CHARLES DICKENS

❧

Alice began to remember that she was a Pawn, and that it would soon be time for her to move.

LEWIS CARROLL

❧

All beginnings are hard. . . . Especially a beginning that you make by yourself. That's the hardest beginning of all.

CHAIM POTOK
In the Beginning

❧

Sometimes I find myself daydreaming about radical changes, new beginnings and great conversions. Yet I know that I must be patient. . . .

HENRI NOUWEN
In Memoriam

ACHIEVEMENT

'Tis God gives skill,
But not without men's hands: He could not
    make
Antonio Stradivari's violins
Without Antonio.

GEORGE ELIOT

God does not require that each individual shall
have capacity for everything.

RICHARD ROTHE

No one has enough talent to do everything well.
Those who achieve greatly understand this early in
life, select one area of interest, and commit all their
personal resources to that one grand obsession.

CHARLES PAUL CONN
Making It Happen

The disciplined person is the person who can do
what needs to be done when it needs to be done.
The mark of a championship basketball team is a
team that can score the points when they are

needed. Most of us can get the ball in the hoop eventually but we can't do it when it is needed.

RICHARD FOSTER
Celebration of Discipline

&

Let us then be up and doing,
With a heart for any fate;
Still achieving, still pursuing,
Learn to labor and to wait.

HENRY WADSWORTH LONGFELLOW

&

Ah, but a man's reach should exceed his grasp,
Or what's a Heaven for?

ROBERT BROWNING

&

Duty makes us do things well, but love makes us do them beautifully.

PHILLIPS BROOKS

ACTIONS

The birds grew silent, because their history laid hold on them, compelling them to turn their words into deeds, and keep eggs warm, and hunt for worms.

GEORGE MACDONALD

What we plant in the soil of contemplation we shall reap in the harvest of action.

MEISTER ECKHART

Our deeds determine us, as much as we determine our deeds.

GEORGE ELIOT

The greatest pleasure I know is to do a good action by stealth, and to have it found out by accident.

CHARLES LAMB

A watched pot never boils.

ELIZABETH GASKELL

Perform every action as though it were your last.

MARCUS AURELIUS

AGING

You are . . . as young as your hope, as old as your despair.

ANONYMOUS

Now, you're not going to get me to declare when growing *up* stops and growing *old* starts—not on your life!

CHARLES SWINDOLL
Growing Strong in the Seasons of Life

Young men think old men are fools; but old men know young men are the fools.

GEORGE CHAPMAN

When I was young I was sure of everything; in a few years, having been mistaken a thousand times, I was not half so sure of most things as I was before; at present, I am hardly sure of anything but what God has revealed to me.

JOHN WESLEY

When I was young I was sure of everything; in a few years, having been mistaken a thousand

At 20 years of age the will reigns; at 30 the wit; at 40 the judgment.

BENJAMIN FRANKLIN

The old believe everything: the middle-aged suspect everything: the young know everything.

OSCAR WILDE

The old woman I shall become will be quite different from the woman I am now. Another *I* is beginning, and so far I have not had to complain of her.

GEORGE SAND

You are young, you are on your way up, when you cannot imagine how you will save yourself from death by boredom until dinner, until bed, until the next day arrives to be outwaited, and then, slow slap, the next. You . . . think that life by its mere appalling length is a feat of endurance for which you haven't the strength.

But momentum propels you over the crest. Imperceptibly, you start down. When do the days start to blur and then, breaking your heart, the seasons? The cards click faster in the spokes. . . . The blur of cards makes one long sound like a bomb's whine, the whine of many bombs, and you know your course is fatal.

ANNIE DILLARD
Teaching a Stone to Talk

&

In seed time learn, in harvest teach, in winter enjoy.

WILLIAM BLAKE

&

O Lord, let me not live to be useless.

BISHOP STRATFORD

&

Like the eagle He renews
The vigor of my youth.

JAMES MONTGOMERY

AMBITIONS

I believe I have spent half my life waiting for
God to catch up with me.

PHILLIPS BROOKS

Most people would succeed in small things if
they were not troubled with great ambitions.

HENRY WADSWORTH LONGFELLOW

Hasten slowly.

AUGUSTUS CAESAR

We never know how high we are
Till we are asked to rise
And then if we are true to plan
Our statures touch the skies—. . . .

EMILY DICKINSON

⊷

On what strange stuff Ambition feeds!

ELIZA COOK

⊷

Make it your ambition to lead a quiet life, to mind your own business and to work with your hands, just as we told you, so that your daily life may win the respect of outsiders and so that you will not be dependent on anybody.

1 Thessalonians 4:11, 12

ANGER

It is healthier to view anger as a normal human emotion that everyone must learn to accept and deal with in daily life than to pretend that it doesn't exist in the life of a healthy believer. The fact that you experience anger in no way implies that you should consider yourself less spiritual than others.

RICHARD D. DOBBINS
Your Spiritual and Emotional Power

Love . . . is not easily angered.

1 Corinthians 13:4, 5

For as churning the milk produces butter,
    and as twisting the nose produces blood,
    so stirring up anger produces strife.

Proverbs 30:33

A sharp tongue is the only edge tool that grows keener with constant use.

WASHINGTON IRVING

Petty ills try the temper worse than great ones.

ELLEN WOOD

Better a patient man than a warrior,
   a man who controls his temper than one
   who takes a city.

Proverbs 16:32

Beware the fury of a patient man.

JOHN DRYDEN

BOOKS

Of making many books there is no end, and
much study wearies the body.

Ecclesiastes 12:12

The great drawback in new books is that they prevent our reading the old ones.

JOSEPH JOUBERT

≈ֆ

Never read any book that is not a year old.

RALPH WALDO EMERSON

≈ֆ

There are the men who pretend to understand a book by scouting through the index: as if a traveler should go about to describe a palace when he had seen nothing but the privy.

JONATHAN SWIFT

≈ֆ

Books are to be called for and supplied on the assumption that the process of reading is not a half-sleep, but in the highest sense an exercise, a gymnastic struggle; that the reader is to do something for himself.

WALT WHITMAN

≈ֆ

Books think for me.

CHARLES LAMB

≈ֆ

Reading is sometimes an ingenious device for avoiding thought.

ARTHUR HELPS

Books are good enough in their own way, but they are a mighty bloodless substitute for life.

ROBERT LOUIS STEVENSON

CALLING

To serve the present age,
My calling to fulfill—
O may it all my pow'rs engage
To do my Master's will.

CHARLES WESLEY

We can live any way we want. People take vows of poverty, chastity, and obedience—even of silence—by choice. The thing is to stalk your calling in a certain skilled and supple way, to locate the most tender and live spot and plug into that pulse. This is yielding, not fighting. A weasel doesn't "attack" anything; a weasel lives as he's meant to, yielding at every moment to the perfect freedom of single necessity.

I think it would be well, and proper, and obedient, and pure, to grasp your one necessity and not let it go, to dangle from it limp wherever it takes you.

ANNIE DILLARD
Teaching a Stone to Talk

∽§

The work of a Beethoven, and the work of a charwoman, become spiritual on precisely the same condition, that of being offered to God, of being done humbly "as to the Lord." This does not, of course, mean that it is for anyone a mere toss-up whether he should sweep rooms or compose symphonies. A mole must dig to the glory of God and a cock must crow.

C. S. LEWIS
The Weight of Glory

CHANGE

There is a time for everything,
and a season for every activity under heaven.

Ecclesiastes 3:1

Events that a few years ago kept me totally preoccupied have now become vague memories; conflicts that a few months ago seemed so crucial in my life now seem futile and hardly worth the energy; inner turmoil that robbed me of my sleep only a few weeks ago has now become a strange emotion of the past; books that filled me with amazement a few days ago now do not seem as important; thoughts which kept my mind captive only a few hours ago, have now lost their power and have been replaced by others.

HENRI NOUWEN
A Cry for Mercy

Life: It's subject to change without notice.

EVELYN BENCE

"Remember the lobster." At a certain point in a lobster's growth, he discards his outer, protective shell and is vulnerable to all of his enemies. This continues until he grows a new "house" in which to live. Change is normal in life.

DENIS WAITLEY
Seeds of Greatness

∽§

We are free to change. The process of that change is always a good story, but it is never a neat formula.

EUGENE PETERSON
Traveling Light

∽§

But the biggest problem of map-making is not that we have to start from scratch, but that if our maps are to be accurate we have to continually revise them. The world itself is constantly changing. Glaciers come, glaciers go. Cultures come, cultures go. There is too little technology, there is too much technology. Even more dramatically, the vantage point from which we view the world is constantly and quite rapidly changing. When we are children we are dependent, powerless. As adults we may be powerful. Yet in illness or an infirm old age we may become powerless and dependent again. . . . The process of making revisions, particularly major revisions, is painful, sometimes excruciatingly painful.

M. SCOTT PECK
The Road Less Traveled

❧

Basically, we really don't like to change. It's like shopping for a new pair of shoes when the old ones are so comfortable. The new shoes fit, but they are so stiff. They don't feel like the old shoes. But we start wearing the new shoes and with time they start to soften and adjust to our feet. And soon they feel better than the old shoes.

DAVID STOOP
Self-Talk

❧

Change of opinion is often only the progress of sound thought and growing knowledge; and though sometimes regarded as an inconsistency, it is but the noble inconsistency natural to a mind ever ready for growth and expansion of thought, and that never fears to follow where truth and duty may lead the way.

TRYON EDWARDS

~§

There is a certain relief in change, even though it be from bad to worse; as I have found in travelling in a stagecoach, that it is often a comfort to shift one's position and be bruised in a new place.

WASHINGTON IRVING

~§

The novel we sit down to write, and the one we end up writing may be very different, just as the Jesus we grasp and the Jesus who grasps us may also differ.

MADELEINE L'ENGLE
Walking on Water

~§

. . . the Father of the heavenly lights . . . does not change like shifting shadows.

JAMES 1:17

CHARACTER

Reputation is what you *think* I am, but character is what God and I *know* I am.

WARREN W. WIERSBE

Why Us?

Happiness is not the end of life; character is.

HENRY WARD BEECHER

Conscience is condensed character.

ANONYMOUS

It is as hard for the good to suspect evil, as it is for the bad to suspect good.

CICERO

A talent is formed in stillness, a character in the world's torrent.

JOHANN WOLFGANG VON GOETHE

Greatness after all, in spite of its name, appears to be not so much a certain size as a certain quality in human lives. It may be present in lives whose range is very small.

PHILLIPS BROOKS

⋖

Strength of character may be acquired at work, but beauty of character is learned at home.

HENRY DRUMMOND

⋖

Whatever disgrace we may have deserved, it is almost always in our power to re-establish our character.

TITUS MACCIUS PLAUTUS

⋖

We know of but one safe rule: read the life of Jesus with attention—study it—inquire earnestly of yourself, "What sort of person, in thought, in feeling, in action was my Saviour?"

HARRIET BEECHER STOWE

⋖

Your attitude should be the same as that of Christ Jesus.

Philippians 2:5

⋖

Give us constancy and steadiness of purpose, that our thoughts may not be fleeting, fond and ineffectual, but that we may perform all things with an unmovable mind, to the glory of thy holy name.

LUDOVICUS VIVES

CHILDHOOD

Backward, turn backward, O Time, in your
    flight,
Make me a child again just for tonight!

ELIZABETH AKERS ALLEN

The future is always a fairy land to the young.

GEORGE AUGUSTUS SALA

The dullest of us knows how memory can transfigure: how

often some momentary glimpse of beauty in
   boyhood is

                    a whisper
Which memory will warehouse as a shout.

                            C. S. LEWIS
                     Letters to Malcolm

As the scent to the rose, are those memories to
me.

                           AMELIA C. WELBY

When I was a child, I talked like a child, I
thought like a child, I reasoned like a child. When
I became a man, I put childish ways behind me.

                       1 Corinthians 13:11

The Child is father of the Man.

                     WILLIAM WORDSWORTH

CHOICES

It is better to make a mistake in an honest choice than never to choose at all.

PAUL TOURNIER
The Meaning of Persons

The Scriptures confirm that sometimes God does give direct guidance by the Holy Spirit. But if not, he does not allow "wrong" choices to go unredeemed. It can't be otherwise. If not, who would be willing to choose when faced by two paths at a fork in the road? We would be paralyzed with fear of making the wrong choice. Or having finally made a choice, we would live always with the agonizing possibility that the other path might have been better.

So in grace, God redeems the choices of his children.

STAN MOONEYHAM
Traveling Hopefully

We can try to avoid making choices by doing nothing, but even that is a decision. By doing nothing, we have passively chosen not to act. That isn't a very effective way to manage our lives.

GARY COLLINS
Getting Your Life Out of Neutral

❧

Do not say that such and such an activity does not interest you before you have tried it.

PAUL TOURNIER
Learn to Grow Old

❧

The difficulty in life is the choice.

GEORGE MOORE

❧

There is a story of a tiger cub that was brought up among goats. One day he got lost in the jungle and ran into a big strong tiger who took one look at him, saw him acting like a goat, and with one cuff of his paw knocked him halfway across the jungle.

I meet a tiger in myself who is not familiar, who

says "Choose!" and knocks me halfway across the jungle.

THOMAS MERTON
Conjectures of a Guilty Bystander

❧

We do well to believe less than we are told, and to keep a wary eye on our impulses; whatever it is, we should think the matter over slowly and carefully, referring it to God.

THOMAS À KEMPIS

❧

On the first page of the Bible we read that God creates life; two pages later man and woman choose death.

EUGENE PETERSON
Traveling Light

❧

I have set before you life and death, blessings and curses. Now choose life.

Deuteronomy 30:19

CONFESSION

If we confess our sins, he is faithful and just and will forgive us our sins and purify us from all unrighteousness. If we claim we have not sinned, we make him out to be a liar and his word has no place in our lives.

1 John 1:9, 10

Why does not man confess his vices? Because he is yet in them. It is for a waking man to tell his dream.

SENECA

We have left undone those things which we ought to have done; and we have done those things which we ought not to have done.

Book of Common Prayer

An honest confession is good for the soul, but bad for the reputation.

ANONYMOUS

Confession is so difficult a Discipline for us partly because we view the believing community as a fellowship of saints before we see it as a fellowship of sinners. We come to feel that everyone else has advanced so far into holiness that we are isolated and alone in our sin.

RICHARD FOSTER
Celebration of Discipline

જ&

God hath promised pardon to him that repenteth, but he hath not promised repentance to him that sinneth.

SAINT ANSELM

જ&

The confession of evil works is the first beginning of good works.

SAINT AUGUSTINE

જ&

Repentance may begin instantly, but reformation often requires a sphere of years.

HENRY WARD BEECHER

જ&

He who knows his own weakness is greater than he who sees the angels.

ISAAC OF NINEVEH

CONSCIENCE

. . . to thine own self be true,
And it must follow as the night the day
Thou canst not then be false to any man.

WILLIAM SHAKESPEARE

Cowardice asks, Is it safe? Experience asks, Is it politic? Vanity asks, Is it popular? but Conscience asks, Is it right?

WILLIAM MORLEY PUNSHON

Labour to keep alive in your breast that little spark of celestial fire, called conscience.

GEORGE WASHINGTON

Conscience is the voice of the soul, the passions are the voice of the body.

JEAN JACQUES ROUSSEAU

❧

If we see cruelty or wrong that we have the power to stop, and do nothing, we make ourselves sharers in the guilt.

ANNA SEWELL

❧

Ah, how steadily do they who are guilty shrink from reproof!

AMELIA JENKS BLOOMER

❧

When people's consciences prick them, sometimes they get angry with other people, which is very silly, and only makes matters worse.

DINAH MULOCK CRAIK

❧

A good conscience is a continual Christmas.

BENJAMIN FRANKLIN

❧

I desire so to conduct the affairs of this administration that if at the end, when I come to lay down the reins of power, I have lost every other friend on earth, I shall at least have one friend left, and that friend shall be down inside of me.

ABRAHAM LINCOLN

⋅≼

My conscience is clear, but that does not make me innocent. It is the Lord who judges me.

1 Corinthians 4:4

CONVERSATION

⋅≼

I wish the creatures wouldn't be so easily offended!

LEWIS CARROLL

⋅≼

The more you say, the less people remember. The fewer the words, the greater the profit.

FRANCOIS DE SALIGNAC DE
LA MOTHE FENELON

⋅≼

When you have nothing to say, say nothing.

CHARLES CALEB COLTON

The silence often of pure innocence
Persuades when speaking fails.

WILLIAM SHAKESPEARE

The small-talk of everyday life can be a genuine road towards contact, a way of getting to know somebody, a prelude to more profound exchanges, a simple and natural approach. But, let us admit it, it is also often used as a means of avoiding personal contact. It is like a prologue that goes on so long that the play never begins. It allows us to be friendly and interesting with people without touching on subjects that would compel us to enter into real dialogue.

PAUL TOURNIER
The Meaning of Persons

Two may talk together under the same roof for many years, yet never really meet; and two others at first speech are old friends.

MARY CATHERWOOD

It is necessary for me to . . . endeavor to speak truth in every instance; to give nobody expectations that are not likely to be answered, but aim at sincerity in every word and action—the most amiable excellence in a rational being.

BENJAMIN FRANKLIN

That truth which is not charitable proceeds from a charity which is not true.

SAINT FRANCIS DE SALES

It is equally an error to believe all men or no man.

SENECA

Never tell all that you know, or do all that you can, or believe all that you hear.

Portuguese Proverb

By all means tell people, when you are busy about something that must be done, that you cannot spare the time for them except they want you upon something of yet more pressing necessity; but *tell* them, and do not get rid of them by the use of the instrument commonly called *the cold shoulder*. It is a wicked instrument.

GEORGE MACDONALD

᪥

The cruelest lies are often told in silence.

ROBERT LOUIS STEVENSON

᪥

With the tongue we praise our Lord and Father, and with it we curse men, who have been made in God's likeness. . . . My brothers, this should not be.

James 3:9, 10

᪥

I resolve to speak ill of no man whatever, not even in a matter of truth; but rather by some means excuse the faults I hear charged upon others, and upon proper occasions speak all the good I know of every body.

BENJAMIN FRANKLIN

᪥

A compliment is something like a kiss through a veil.

VICTOR HUGO

The only way to speak the truth is to speak lovingly.

HENRY DAVID THOREAU

COURAGE

Those who hope in the Lord
will renew their strength.
They will soar on wings like eagles;
they will run and not grow weary,
they will walk and not be faint.

Isaiah 40:31

Our God meets us just where we are. But He does not leave us there. There is power in the word of a King to effect what it commands. In the *Fear not* of our God, repeated from Genesis to Revelation, there is power to give us just what we lack at that moment.

AMY CARMICHAEL
Whispers of His Power

❧

Ye fearful saints, fresh courage take;
The clouds ye so much dread
Are big with mercy, and shall break
In blessings on your head.

WILLIAM COWPER

❧

No man can answer for his courage who has never been in danger.

FRANCOIS DUC DE LA ROCHEFOUCAULD

❧

Any coward can fight a battle when he's sure of winning; but give me the man who has pluck to fight when he's sure of losing. That's my way, sir; and there are many victories worse than a defeat.

GEORGE ELIOT

❧

Not every man is so great a coward as he thinks he is—nor yet so good a Christian.

ROBERT LOUIS STEVENSON

ॐ

A great deal of talent is lost in this world for the want of a little courage.

SYDNEY SMITH

ॐ

Do not pray for tasks equal to your powers. Pray for powers equal to your tasks.

PHILLIPS BROOKS

ॐ

Give me the courage to show the dove in a world so full of serpents.

HENRI NOUWEN
A Cry for Mercy

ॐ

Be like the bird, who
Halting in his flight
On limb too slight
Feels it give way beneath him,

Yet sings
Knowing he hath wings.

VICTOR HUGO

DEATH

In every parting scene there is an image of death.

GEORGE ELIOT

All my possessions for a moment of time.

Last words of Queen Elizabeth I

I depart from life as from an inn, and not as from my home.

CICERO

Here lie I, Martin Elginbrodde:
Have mercy on my soul, Lord God,

As I would do, were I Lord God
and You were Martin Elginbrodde.
                    Epitaph in Elgin Cathedral

᭝

If I thought I was going to die tomorrow, I
should nevertheless plant a tree today.

STEPHEN GIRARD

᭝

Death has been swallowed up in victory. . . .
Where, O death, is thy sting?

1 Corinthians 15:54, 55

᭝

I suppose in looking at compost I am looking at
a sign of the resurrection, of life proceeding out of
death. But I have a hard time accepting the
analogy, for it is badly flawed. In nature the life
that rises out of the dead is never new life for the
dead; it is always merely another life feeding on the
one that died. The resurrection begins a life
unimaginable within the confines of nature.

JOHN LEAX
In Season and Out

DEPRESSION

⤳

Why are you downcast, O my soul?
Why so disturbed within me?

Psalms 43:5

⤳

Depression, that serpent of despair, slithers
silently through the soul's back door.

CHARLES SWINDOLL
Growing Strong in the Seasons of Life

⤳

What we call despair is often only the painful
eagerness of unfed hope.

GEORGE ELIOT

⤳

Beware of desperate steps. The darkest day, live
till tomorrow, will have passed away.

WILLIAM COWPER

⤳

As the farthest reach of our love for each other is
loving our enemies, as the farthest reach of God's
love for us is loving us at our most unlovable and

unlovely, so the farthest reach of our love for God
is loving him when in almost every way that
matters we can neither see him nor hear him . . .
when the worst of the wilderness for us is the fear
that he has forsaken us if indeed he exists at all.

FREDERICK BUECHNER
A Room Called Remember

In you, O Lord, I have taken refuge. . . .
Turn your ear to me,
   come quickly to my rescue;
be my rock of refuge,
   a strong fortress to save me.

Psalms 31:1, 2

. . . my soul is downcast within me.
Yet this I call to mind
   and therefore I have hope:
Because of the Lord's great love we are not
consumed,
   for his compassions never fail.
They are new every morning;
   great is your faithfulness.

Lamentations 3:20–23

There is another very safe and simple way of escape when the dull mood begins to gather round one, and that is to turn as promptly and as strenuously as one can to whatever work one can at the moment do. If the energy, the clearness, the power of intention, is flagging in us, if we cannot do our best work, still let us do what we can—for we can always do something; if not high work, then low work; if not vivid and spiritual work, then the plain, needful drudgery.

FRANCIS PAGET

DOUBT

The great artists keep us from frozenness, from smugness, from thinking that the truth is in us, rather than in God, in Christ our Lord. They help us to know that we are often closer to God in our doubts than in our certainties, that it is all right to be like the small child who constantly asks: Why? Why? Why?

MADELEINE L'ENGLE
Walking on Water

You call for faith:
I show you doubt, to prove that faith exists.
The more of doubt, the stronger faith, I say,
If faith o'ercomes doubt.

ROBERT BROWNING

If a man will begin with certainties, he shall end in doubts; but if he will be content to begin with doubts, he shall end in certainties.

FRANCIS BACON

Doubters invert the metaphor and insist that they need faith as big as a mountain in order to move a mustard seed.

ANONYMOUS

Let me not linger in ignorance and doubt, but enlighten and support me.

SAMUEL JOHNSON

It is never worth while to make rents in a garment for the sake of mending them, nor to create doubts in order to show how cleverly we can quiet them.

CHARLES HADDON SPURGEON

I do believe; help me overcome my unbelief!
Mark 9:24

DREAMS

Some things wilt thou not one day turn to
dreams?
Some dreams wilt thou not one day turn to
fact?
The thing that painful, more than should be,
seems,
Shall not thy sliding years with them re-
tract—
Shall fair realities not counteract?
The thing that was well dreamed of bliss and
joy—
Wilt thou not breathe thy life into the toy?

GEORGE MACDONALD

It can't be Christmas all the time.

MARGARET SIDNEY

Much dreaming and many words are meaning-
less.

Ecclesiastes 5:7

You are either the captive or the captain of your thoughts. You can resign yourself to mediocrity or you can dare to dream of conquering outer space.

DENIS WAITLEY
Psychology of Winning

Far away there in the sunshine are my highest aspirations. I may not reach them, but I can look up and see their beauty, believe in them, and try to follow where they lead.

LOUISA MAY ALCOTT

Hitch your wagon to a star.

RALPH WALDO EMERSON

Well, I am glad of my dream, for I hope ere long to see it fulfilled, to the making of me laugh again.

JOHN BUNYAN

Happiness is no vague dream, of that I now feel certain.

GEORGE SAND

Your dreams must never be so important to y
that other people become only fodder to feed them.

CALVIN MILLE

Becoming

EXPERIENCE

Experience has no text books nor proxies. She demands that her pupils answer her roll-call personally.

MINNA ANTRIM

Experience keeps a dear school; but fools will learn in no other, and scarce in that; for it is true, we may give advice, but we cannot give conduct.

BENJAMIN FRANKLIN

Not all the possible descriptions of headlong love will make me comprehend the *delirium,* if I have never had a fit of it.

JOHN HENRY NEWMAN

❧

Experience is the name everyone gives to their mistakes.

OSCAR WILDE

❧

Experience is a good teacher, but she sends in terrific bills.

MINNA ANTRIM

❧

Experience is a jewel, and it had need be so, for it is often purchased at an infinite rate.

WILLIAM SHAKESPEARE

❧

Experience is by industry achieved, and perfected by the swift course of time.

WILLIAM SHAKESPEARE

❧

No one is so eager to gain new experience as he who doesn't know how to make use of the old ones.

MARIE EBNER VON ESCHENBACH

FAITH

Now faith is being sure of what we hope for and certain of what we do not see.

Hebrews 11:1

The righteous will live by faith.

Galatians 3:11

Faith is a way of looking at what is seen and understanding it in a new sense. Faith is a way of looking at what there is to be seen in the world and in ourselves and hoping, trusting, believing against

all evidence to the contrary that beneath the surface
we see there is vastly more that we cannot see.

FREDERICK BUECHNER
A Room Called Remember

≈§

Live by faith until you have faith.

PETER BOEHLER

≈§

The mere swallowing of food is not enough
unless it be assimilated and digested; yet it is a
necessary condition of digestion. So with our
beliefs; we swallow them wholesale by an act of
extrinsic faith based on the word of others; and
such faith is like the prop that supports a plant till
it strikes root downwards and becomes self-
supporting. They are not ours fully save in the
measure that we have worked them into the fabric
of our life and thought.

GEORGE TYRRELL

≈§

It is faith that is expected of you and honest
living, not profound understanding and deep
knowledge of the mysteries of God.

THOMAS À KEMPIS

≈§

Faith goes up the stairs that love has made and looks out of the windows which hope has opened.

CHARLES HADDON SPURGEON

Faith is the antiseptic of the soul.

WALT WHITMAN

Faith needs her daily bread.

DINAH MULOCK CRAIK

Lord, give us faith that right makes might.

ABRAHAM LINCOLN

Reason is our Soules left hand, Faith her right,
By these we reach divinity.

JOHN DONNE

Meanwhile (don't I know) the trouble is that relying on God has to begin all over again every day as if nothing had yet been done.

C. S. LEWIS

Letters of C. S. Lewis

⊸§

Sufficient unto the Day Is the Faith Thereof
Like manna from heaven
what you need for tomorrow
will be yours for the taking at dawn,
but will rot and grow wormy
if hoarded on Wednesday for Thursday.

EVELYN BENCE

Leaving Home

From *Leaving Home* by Evelyn Bence, copyright © 1982. Used by permission of the Westminster Press.

⊸§

I have held many things in my hands, and have lost them all; but whatever I have placed in God's hands, that I still possess.

MARTIN LUTHER

FEAR

There is a virtuous fear which is the effect of faith, and a vicious fear which is the product of doubt and distrust. The former leads to hope as relying on God, in whom we believe; the latter inclines to despair, as not relying upon God, in whom we do not believe. Persons of the one character fear to lose God; those of the other character fear to find him.

BLAISE PASCAL

"But is not any sort of fear," continued the tempter, "a proof that thou dost not believe?" I desired my Master to answer for me, and opened His Book upon those words of St. Paul, "Without were fightings, within were fears." Then, inferred I, well may fears be within me; but I must go on, and tread them under my feet.

JOHN WESLEY

He has not learned the lesson of life who does not every day surmount a fear.

RALPH WALDO EMERSON

No endeavour is fruitful without fear. There is no good actor who does not have to contend with stage-fright.

PAUL TOURNIER
The Strong and the Weak

❧

There is no life without desire; there is no desire without fear; one cannot desire a thing without being afraid of not obtaining it.

PAUL TOURNIER
The Strong and the Weak

From *The Strong and the Weak*, by Paul Tournier, copyright © 1976. Used by permission of the Westminster Press.

❧

It is a miserable state of mind to have few things to desire, and many things to fear.

FRANCIS BACON

❧

Find successful "role models" that you can pattern yourself after. When you meet a "mastermind," become a "master mime" and learn all you can about how he or she succeeded. This is especially true with things you fear. Find someone

who has conquered what you fear, and get edu-
cated.

DENIS WAITLEY
Seeds of Greatness

I am never afraid of what I know.

ANNA SEWELL

It may help us to do this, to reflect that the very
person whose opinion we fear may be in equal
dread of ours.

HARRIET BEECHER STOWE

And though this world, with devils filled,
Should threaten to undo us,
We will not fear, for God has willed
His truth to triumph through us.

MARTIN LUTHER

FORGIVENESS

Time heals griefs and quarrels, for we change and are no longer the same persons. Neither the offender nor the offended are any more themselves. It is like a nation which we have provoked, but meet again after two generations. They are still Frenchmen, but not the same.

BLAISE PASCAL

Children begin by loving their parents; as they grow older they judge them, sometimes they forgive them.

OSCAR WILDE

Perhaps it is that slow but inexorable movement outward from the womb of her body, the womb of her home, that we have such a hard time forgiving our mothers for.

VIRGINIA STEM OWENS
A Feast of Families

Good to forget—
Best to forgive!

ROBERT BROWNING

~§

Clara Barton, the founder of the American Red Cross, was reminded one day of a vicious deed that someone had done to her years before. But she acted as if she had never heard of the incident.

"Don't you remember it?" her friend asked.

"No," came Barton's reply. "I distinctly remember forgetting it."

LUIS PALAU
Experiencing God's Forgiveness

~§

And when you stand praying, if you hold anything against anyone, forgive him, so that your Father in heaven may forgive you your sins. But if you do not forgive neither will your Father who is in heaven forgive your sins.

Mark 11:25, 26

~§

Keep what is worth keeping—
And with the breath of kindness
Blow the rest away.

DINAH MULOCK CRAIK

❧

It is easier for the generous to forgive, than for the offender to ask forgiveness.

JAMES THOMSON

FREEDOM

❧

A man is in bondage to whatever he cannot part with that is less than himself.

GEORGE MACDONALD

❧

You cannot have complete freedom unless you deny your own claims entirely. . . . Hold on to the brief saying that sums this up—Leave everything and you will find everything.

THOMAS À KEMPIS

&

Whoever tries to keep his life will lose it, and whoever loses his life will preserve it.

Luke 17:33

&

When I set God at the center of my life, I realize vast freedoms and surprising spontaneities. When I center life in my own will, my freedom diminishes markedly. I live constricted and anxious.

EUGENE PETERSON
Traveling Light

&

A Christian is a perfectly free lord of all, subject to none. A Christian is a perfectly dutiful servant of all, subject to all.

MARTIN LUTHER

&

My yoke is easy and my burden is light.

Matthew 11:30

&

God compels nobody, for He will have no one saved by compulsion. God has given freewill to men that they may choose for themselves, either the good or the bad. Christ said to His disciples, "Will ye go away?" as though He would say, "You are under no compulsion." God forces no one, for love cannot compel, and God's service is, therefore, a thing of complete freedom.

RUFUS JONES

So if the Son sets you free, you will be free indeed.

John 8:36

Stone walls do not a prison make.

RICHARD LOVELACE

FRIENDS

The world is so empty if one thinks only of mountains, rivers, and cities; but to know someone who thinks and feels with us, and who, though distant, is close to us in spirit, this makes the earth for us an inhabited garden.

JOHANN WOLFGANG VON GOETHE

To be a strong hand in the dark to another in the time of need.

HUGO BLACK

A friend is a present you give yourself.

ROBERT LOUIS STEVENSON

The holy passion of Friendship is of so sweet and steady and loyal and enduring a nature that it will last through a whole lifetime, if not asked to lend money.

MARK TWAIN

Business, you know, may bring money, but friendship hardly ever does.

JANE AUSTEN

❧

I lay it down as a fact that if all men knew what others say of them, there would not be four friends in the world.

BLAISE PASCAL

❧

God save me from my friends; I can take care of my enemies.

English Proverb

❧

Kind thoughts are rarer than either kind words or kind deeds. They imply a great deal of thinking about others. This in itself is rare. But they imply also a great deal of thinking about others without the thoughts being criticisms. This is rarer still.

FREDERICK W. FABER

❧

Instead of a gem or a flower, cast the gift of a lovely thought into the heart of a friend.

GEORGE MACDONALD

❧

Forsake not an old friend, for the new is not comparable unto him.

Ecclesiasticus 9:10

ᕒᔖ

We cannot tell the precise moment when friendship is formed. As in filling a vessel drop by drop, there is at last a drop which makes it run over; so in a series of kindnesses there is at last one which makes the heart run over.

JAMES BOSWELL

ᕒᔖ

If we build on a sure foundation in friendship, we must love our friends for their sakes rather than for our own.

CHARLOTTE BRONTË

ᕒᔖ

If a man does not make new acquaintances as he advances through life, he will soon find himself alone. A man, Sir, should keep his friendship in constant repair.

SAMUEL JOHNSON

ᕒᔖ

What a Friend we have in Jesus,
All our sins and griefs to bear!
What a privilege to carry
Everything to God in prayer!
O what peace we often forfeit,
O what needless pain we bear,
All because we do not carry
Everything to God in prayer!

JOSEPH SCRIVEN

FUTURE

I know of no way of judging the future but by
the past.

PATRICK HENRY

My garden has taught me to think ahead. For it
to be fruitful, I must plan. I must build soil, plant,
and nurture what I have planted. It has also taught

me to hold the harvest lightly. Over the course of a
season I can lose a crop to spring rains that rot the
seed, slugs that eat new shoots, rabbits that eat
everything, hail that breaks the strong, and drought
that withers the weak. I can lose a crop because of my
ignorance or my carelessness. Until I have the fruit
in storage, where it can also spoil, I live with un-
certainty. I do my best, work faithfully, and hope.

JOHN LEAX
In Season and Out

❧

Tomorrow is, ah, whose?

DINAH MULOCK CRAIK

❧

Now listen, you who say, "Today or tomorrow
we will go to this or that city, spend a year there,
carry on business and make money." Why, you do
not even know what will happen tomorrow.

James 4:13, 14

❧

God does not paint by numbers.

PHILIP YANCEY
Guidance

❧

I expect some new phases of life this summer, and shall try to get the honey from each moment.

LUCY STONE

～ξ

There is not a heart but has its moments of longing, yearning for something better, nobler, holier than it knows now.

HENRY WARD BEECHER

～ξ

God will not suffer man to have a knowledge of things to come; for if he had prescience of his prosperity, he would be careless; and if understanding of his adversity, he would be despairing and senseless.

SAINT AUGUSTINE

～ξ

Nowhere in the Bible does it say that God is going to give you a plan for your entire life. He never said that He would lay out His plan for your life in cinemascope so you can view it in its entirety. What He does promise is to lead you *as*

you go; to direct you day by day; to show you His
will hour by hour.

TONY CAMPOLO
You Can Make A Difference

❧

"I know the plans I have for you," declares the
Lord, "plans to prosper you and not to harm you,
plans to give you hope and a future."

Jeremiah 29:11

❧

Seek not to know the future. Mercifully I veil it
from you.

Faith is too priceless a possession to be sacrificed
in order to purchase knowledge. But Faith itself is
based on a knowledge of Me.

TWO LISTENERS
God Calling

❧

Peace, perfect peace, our future all unknown?
Jesus we know, and He is on the throne.

EDWARD BICKERSTETH

GENEROSITY

A man there was, though some did count
   him mad,
The more he cast away the more he had.

JOHN BUNYAN

If I give all I possess to the poor and surrender
my body to the flames, but have not love, I gain
nothing.

1 Corinthians 13:3

The freedom to give is often vitiated by the
moral disease of Afghanistanitus, the idea that the
real opportunities for significant acts of giving are
in faraway places or extreme situations.

EUGENE PETERSON
Traveling Light

What seems to be generosity is often no more
than disguised ambition, which overlooks a small
interest in order to secure a great one.

FRANCOIS DUC DE LA ROCHEFOUCAULD

No gift is poor if it expresses the true love of the giver.

TWO LISTENERS
God Calling

Not what we give, but what we share,
For the gift without the giver is bare.

JAMES RUSSELL LOWELL

He who gives what he would as readily throw away, gives without generosity; for the essence of generosity is in self-sacrifice.

SIR HENRY TAYLOR

We cannot be generous without repressing our egoism, or give way to egoism without repressing our generosity.

PAUL TOURNIER
The Adventure of Living

Let him who would learn how to give, first learn how to receive.

KENNETH L. WILSON
All Things Considered

Even if it feels uncomfortable, accept all the compliments, gifts and values offered by others for whatever reason they offer them by simply saying, "Thank you." Get that deep, down inside feeling of your own worth.

DENIS WAITLEY
Psychology of Winning

⋙

He that will only Give, and not Receive,
Enslaves the Person whom he would Relieve.

SIR SAMUEL TUKE

⋙

Freely you have received, freely give.

Matthew 10:8

⋙

Give not Saint Peter so much, to leave Saint Paul nothing.

GEORGE HERBERT

⋙

Do all the good you can,
By all the means you can,
In all the ways you can,

In all the places you can,
At all the times you can,
To all the people you can,
As long as ever you can.

JOHN WESLEY

⌇

Remember this: Whoever sows sparingly will also reap sparingly, and whoever sows generously will also reap generously. Each man should give what he has decided in his heart to give, not reluctantly or under compulsion, for God loves a cheerful giver.

2 Corinthians 9:6, 7

GOALS
⌇

To be what we are, and to become what we are capable of becoming, is the only end of life.

ROBERT LOUIS STEVENSON

⌇

If we could first know where we were, and whither we are tending, we could better judge what to do, and how to do it.

ABRAHAM LINCOLN

◦§

The great danger facing all of us . . . is not that we shall make an absolute failure of life, nor that we shall fall into outright viciousness, nor that we shall be terribly unhappy, nor that we shall feel that life has no meaning at all—not these things. The danger is that we may fail to perceive life's greatest meaning, fall short of its highest good, miss its deepest and most abiding happiness, be unable to render the most needed service, be unconscious of life ablaze with the light of the Presence of God—and be content to have it so— that is the danger. . . . That is what one prays one's friends may be spared—satisfaction with life that falls short of the best.

PHILLIPS BROOKS

◦§

One wants to be *very* something, *very* great, *very* heroic; or if not that, then at least very stylish and very fashionable. It is this everlasting mediocrity that bores me.

HARRIET BEECHER STOWE

⇜ॐ

A drifting boat always drifts down-stream.

CHARLES PARKHURST

⇜ॐ

Looking through a peephole is no way to stay motivated when you're moving toward a goal.

The big view is important. It takes big dreams—big goals—big rewards—big faith—to keep us moving through obstacles and fatigue and discouragement. To maintain momentum requires constantly reminding ourselves what we are working toward.

CHARLES PAUL CONN
Making It Happen

⇜ॐ

Achievement of great goals must always occur in the face of misunderstanding and often outright criticism. . . . Winston Churchill was disgraced by the failures of British naval policy during World War I and was so devastated by critics that he was

generally thought to be finished as a career politi-
cian. But he came back, at the age of sixty-six, to
become Prime Minister of England and carve his
mark as one of the greatest leaders of this century.

CHARLES PAUL CONN
Making It Happen

I press on toward the goal to win the prize for
which God has called me heavenward in Christ
Jesus.

Philippians 3:14

GRACE

My grace is sufficient for you, for my power is
made perfect in weakness.

2 Corinthians 12:9

I see that grace groweth best in winter.

SAMUEL RUTHERFORD

I have never found anyone, however religious and devout, who did not sometimes experience withdrawal of grace, or feel a lessening of devotion.

THOMAS À KEMPIS

✌

What is grace? I know until you ask me; when you ask me, I do not know.

SAINT AUGUSTINE

✌

O Lord, I need your grace so much if I am to start anything good, or go on with it, or bring it to completion. Without grace, I have no power to do anything—but nothing is beyond my power, if your grace gives strength to me.

THOMAS À KEMPIS

✌

There is, immediately in front of us, an appointed task, a call: some difficult, clear, utterly simple thing the Lord is asking us to do. It is not a general admonition to whoever might happen to be standing about. It is instead an utterly private request whispered, as it were, into each one's ear.

What the Lord is asking me, he is asking no one else. . . .

And I cannot accomplish this thing God asks without grace. The call, this request is completely beyond my grasp, quite impossible—without his help. Yet even as he asks it, he makes it clear that his grace will be poured out. He will give me the power to do what is needed. He will not leave me abandoned or alone. He does not ask the impossible. Our God does not play tricks.

EMILIE GRIFFIN
Clinging

❧

The things, good Lord, that I pray for, give me Thy grace to labor for.

THOMAS MORE

❧

There is no such way to attain to greater measure of grace as for a man to live up to the little grace he has.

PHILLIPS BROOKS

❧

We are suspicious of grace. We are afraid of the very lavishness of the gift.

But a child rejoices in presents!

MADELEINE L'ENGLE
Walking on Water

❧

Where sin increased, grace increased all the more.

Romans 5:20

GRATITUDE

❧

Gratitude is the heart's memory.

French Proverb

❧

Thou hast given so much to us, give us one thing more: a grateful heart.

GEORGE HERBERT

❧

When children are grown, their parents' sacrifices are either fulfilled in an adult intimacy or disappointed by a lack of it. Many grown children continue to be indifferent to what their parents did, and a melancholy aridity, a disappointed silence sets in.

Other children do become aware and begin to say thank you. They begin to do small favors for their parents, not to repay them for their sacrifices—for they cannot—but merely to please them.

TIM STAFFORD
Knowing the Face of God

༚ᢌ

Some people complain because God put thorns on roses, while others praise Him for putting roses among thorns.

ANONYMOUS

ᢌᢓ

In your prayer, do not hesitate to thank the Lord for all that he gives. This is often difficult since we are not always willing to receive some of the "gifts" which make little sense to us. Yet all is a gift from God.

CHRIS ARIDAS
Soundings

ᢌᢓ

What soon grows old? Gratitude.

ARISTOTLE

&

Thanks be to thee,
Lord Jesus Christ,
for all the benefits
which thou hast won for us,
for all the pains and insults
which thou hast borne for us.
O most merciful Redeemer,
Friend and Brother,
may we know thee more clearly,
love thee more dearly,
and follow thee more nearly,
day by day.

RICHARD OF CHICHESTER

GRIEF

Every one can master a grief but he that has it.

WILLIAM SHAKESPEARE

I have something more to do than feel.

CHARLES LAMB

To weep is to make less the depth of grief.

WILLIAM SHAKESPEARE

No bond
In closer union knits two human hearts
Than fellowship in grief.

ROBERT SOUTHEY

Grief melts away
Like snow in May,
As if there were no such cold thing.

GEORGE HERBERT

Time is the great comforter of grief, but the agency by which it works is exhaustion.

LETITIA ELIZABETH LANDON

Earth has no sorrow that Heaven cannot heal.

THOMAS MOORE

GROWTH

All growth that is not towards God
Is growing to decay.

GEORGE MACDONALD

. . . what we call hindrances are really the raw material of spiritual life. As if the fire should call the coal a hindrance!

C. S. LEWIS
They Stand Together

So slow
The growth of what is excellent; so hard
T'attain perfection in this nether world.

WILLIAM COWPER

In the acquisition of a new habit, or the leaving off of an old one, we must take care to launch ourselves with as strong and decided an initiative as possible. Accumulate all the possible circumstances which shall re-enforce the right motives; put yourself assiduously in conditions that encourage the new way; make engagements incompatible with the old. . . .

Could the young but realize how soon they will become mere walking bundles of habits, they would give more heed to their conduct while in the plastic state. We are spinning our own fates, good or evil.

WILLIAM JAMES

Life consists in the alternate process of learning and unlearning, but it is often wiser to unlearn than to learn.

EDWARD GEORGE BULWER-LYTTON

Long ago I discovered that people who refuse to take risks almost never grow. When we struggle with choices and risk making mistakes, we become better and more mature people.

GARY COLLINS
Getting Your Life Out of Neutral

❧

God created man something on the order of a rubber band. A rubber band is made to stretch. When it is not being stretched, it is small and relaxed; but as long as it remains in that shape, it is not doing what it was made to do. When it stretches, it is enlarged; it becomes tense and dynamic, and it does what it was made to do. God created *you* to stretch.

CHARLES PAUL CONN
Making It Happen

HAPPINESS

No one can be perfectly happy till all are happy.

HERBERT SPENCER

Our moments of greatest happiness often come quite unexpectedly, and if we tried to hold on to them or reproduce them, it would be in vain.

PAUL TOURNIER
The Person Reborn

I have observed that when any of us embarks on the pursuit of happiness for ourselves, it eludes us. Often I've asked myself why. It must be because happiness comes to us only as a dividend. When we become absorbed in something demanding and worthwhile above and beyond ourselves, happiness seems to be there as a by-product of the self-giving.

That should not be a startling truth, yet I'm surprised at how few people understand and accept it. Have we made a god of happiness? Have we been brainwashed by ads assuring us "Happiness is . . ."—usually a big, shiny, new gadget?

CATHERINE MARSHALL
A Closer Walk

≈§

If we are fools enough to remain at the mercy of the people who want to sell us happiness, it will be impossible for us ever to be content with anything. How would they profit if we became content? We would no longer need their new product.

The last thing the salesman wants is for the buyer to become content. You are of no use in our affluent society unless you are always just about to grasp what you never have.

THOMAS MERTON
Conjectures of a Guilty Bystander

≈§

I found much to bewilder me in my memories of the long time which had passed since I was nineteen, the age at which I had first begun to search in earnest for truth and wisdom and had promised myself that, once I had found them, I would give up all the vain hopes and mad delusions

which sustained my futile ambitions. I realized
that I was now thirty years old and was still
floundering in the same quagmire, because I was
greedy to enjoy what the world had to offer,
though it only eluded me and wrested my
strength. . . . I longed for a life of happiness but I
was frightened to approach it in its own domain;
and yet, while I fled from it, I still searched for it.

SAINT AUGUSTINE

Good nature is worth more than knowledge,
more than money, more than honour, to the
persons who possess it, and certainly to everybody
who dwells with them, in so far as mere happiness
is concerned.

HENRY WARD BEECHER

Happiness is neither without us nor within us.
It is in God, both without us and within us.

BLAISE PASCAL

Where Christ is cheerfulness will keep breaking
in.

DOROTHY L. SAYERS
The Man Born to Be King

HEAVEN

I would not give one moment of heaven for all the joy and riches of the world, even if it lasted for thousands and thousands of years.

MARTIN LUTHER

It has been more wittily than charitably said that hell is paved with good intentions; they have their place in heaven also.

ROBERT SOUTHEY

After thinking about it the last few days, I'm convinced that heaven's unnecessariness is what makes it important. It's important because it has no relevance to this life. (It does not follow that this life has no relevance to it.) Heaven is simply a glorious, gratuitous extra, totally unnecessary, but totally in character with the extravagant goodness and boundless creativeness of the Maker and Redeemer of this world.

JOHN LEAX
In Season and Out

Rest is reserved for Heaven; on earth we must always struggle between hope and fear.

SAINT FRANCIS DE SALES

In that blessed city no one, in any lower place, shall envy his superior; for no one will ever wish to be that to which he has not been appointed. Together with his reward, each shall have the gift of a great contentment, so as to desire no more than he has got. There we shall rest and see, there we shall see and love, and there we shall all love and praise in the City of God.

SAINT AUGUSTINE

Our Father refreshes us on the journey with some pleasant inns, but will not encourage us to mistake them for Home.

C. S. LEWIS
The Problem of Pain

Now comes the mystery.
Last words of Henry Ward Beecher

HOME

Not many sounds in life, and I include all urban and all rural sounds, exceed in interest a knock on the door.

CHARLES LAMB

When you knock it never is at home.

WILLIAM COWPER

You can't appreciate home till you've left it.

O. HENRY

One always begins to forgive a place as soon as it's left behind.

CHARLES DICKENS

You Can't Go Home Again.

THOMAS WOLFE

Do they miss me at home—do they miss me?
'Twould be an assurance most dear,
To know that this moment some loved one
Were saying, "I wish he were here."

CAROLINE MASON

God is at home. We are in the far country.

MEISTER ECKHART

Ye who are weary, come home.

WILL L. THOMPSON

God, who is our home.

WILLIAM WORDSWORTH

O God, our help in ages past,
Our hope for years to come,
Our shelter from the stormy blast,
And our eternal home!

ISAAC WATTS

HOPE

—— ❧ ——

"Hope" is the thing with feathers—
That perches in the soul—
And sings the tune without the words—
And never stops—at all—

EMILY DICKINSON

❧

Diet books are always in.

ROBERT I. BARR

❧

He who plants a tree
Plants a hope.

LUCY LARCOM

❧

Prayer is a cry of hope.

French Proverb

❧

Hope that is seen is no hope at all. Who hopes
for what he already has? But if we hope for what we
do not yet have, we wait for it patiently.

Romans 8:24, 25

❧

All human wisdom is summed up in two words—wait and hope.

ALEXANDRE DUMAS THE ELDER

"All hope abandon, ye who enter here."

I used to think those grim words that Dante saw above the entrance to the Inferno were placed there to add further misery to sinners consigned to everlasting torment. Faced with the prospect of endless pain, they were being denied even the solace of hope.

But now, on further thought, I wonder if the purpose of the words might have been to protect hell itself, protect it against hope. Those who entered were told to leave hope behind because if even a spark began to glow, all the darkness of hell would not be able to put it out.

And hell could be hell no longer.

ARTHUR GORDON
A Song Called Hope

Don't leave off hoping, or it's no use doing anything. Hope, hope, to the last.

CHARLES DICKENS

᪥

Make my hope
as personal
as my shadow—
but more constant, Lord,
more constant.

EVELYN BENCE
The Promise

᪥

We also rejoice in our sufferings, because we know that suffering produces perseverance; perseverance, character; and character, hope. And hope does not disappoint us.

Romans 5:3–5

᪥

Love . . . always hopes.

1 Corinthians 13:6, 7

᪥

Confident hope breeds inward joy.

CHARLES HADDON SPURGEON

HUMILITY

Lighthouses do not ring bells and fire cannon to call attention to their shining—they just shine.

DWIGHT L. MOODY

Pepper calls attention to itself. That is its business. Salt, on the other hand (unless it is overdone), calls attention to what it salts.

KENNETH L. WILSON
All Things Considered

Humility is the first of the virtues—for other people.

OLIVER WENDELL HOLMES, SR.

Do you wish people to think well of you? Don't speak well of yourself.

BLAISE PASCAL

The true way to be humble is not to stoop until you are smaller than yourself, but to stand at your real height against some higher nature that will show you what the real smallness of your greatness is.

PHILLIPS BROOKS

❧

I do not know what I may appear to the world; but to myself I seem to have been only like a boy playing on the seashore, and diverting myself in now and then finding of a smoother pebble or a prettier shell than ordinary whilst the great ocean of truth lay all undiscovered before me.

ISAAC NEWTON

IMAGINATION

❧

There are no days in life so memorable as those which vibrated to some stroke of the imagination.

RALPH WALDO EMERSON

❧

Bringing imagination to a job does not require a supervisor's approval.

CHERYL FORBES
Imagination

❧

The man who lets himself be bored is even more contemptible than the bore.

SAMUEL BUTLER

❧

Iron rusts from disuse, stagnant water loses its purity and in cold weather becomes frozen; even so does inaction sap the vigors of the mind.

LEONARDO DA VINCI

❧

The imagination of a boy is healthy, and the mature imagination of a man is healthy; but there is a space of life between, in which the soul is in a ferment, the character undecided, the way of life uncertain, the ambition thick-sighted.

JOHN KEATS

INDIVIDUALS

No man is an island entire of itself; every man is a piece of the continent, a part of the main. If a clod be washed away by the sea, Europe is the less, as well as if a promontory were, as well as if a manor of thy friend's or of thine own were. Any man's death diminishes me, because I am involved in mankind, and therefore never send to know for whom the bell tolls; it tolls for thee.

JOHN DONNE

The community stagnates without the impulse of the individual. The impulse dies away without the sympathy of the community.

WILLIAM JAMES

It has always been a favorite idea of mine, that there is so much of the human in every man, that the life of any one individual, however obscure, if really and vividly perceived in all its aspirations, struggles, failures, and successes, would command the interest of all others.

HARRIET BEECHER STOWE

A wonderful fact to reflect upon, that every human creature is constituted to be that profound secret and mystery to every other.

CHARLES DICKENS

≈§

Who in the world am I? Ah, that's the great puzzle!

LEWIS CARROLL

≈§

The resolve is always the same: never to be "thingafied."

RICHARD FOSTER
Money, Sex and Power

≈§

Men go forth to wonder at the height of mountains, the huge waves of the sea, the broad flow of the ocean, the course of the stars—and forget to wonder at themselves.

SAINT AUGUSTINE

JOY

All Joy reminds. It is never a possession, always a desire for something longer ago or further away or still "about to be."

C. S. LEWIS
Surprised by Joy

O Joy that seekest me through pain,
I cannot close my heart to Thee;
I trace the rainbow through the rain,
And feel the promise is not vain
That morn shall tearless be.

GEORGE MATHESON

Weeping may remain for a night,
but rejoicing comes in the morning.

Psalms 30:5

Joys are our wings; sorrows our spurs.

JEAN PAUL RICHTER

A woman giving birth to a child has pain because her time has come; but when her baby is born she forgets the anguish because of her joy that a child is born into the world. So with you: Now is your time of grief, but I will see you again and you will rejoice, and no one will take away your joy.

John 16:21, 22

⋅ξ

Tranquil pleasures last the longest; we are not fitted to bear long the burden of great joys.

CHRISTIAN NESTELL BOVEE

⋅ξ

Words are less needful to sorrow than to joy.

HELEN FISKE HUNT JACKSON

⋅ξ

The working out of this our salvation must be pain, and the handing of it down to them that are below must ever be in pain; but the eternal form of the will of God in and for us, is intensity of bliss.

GEORGE MACDONALD

⋅ξ

Christian joy is not an escape from sorrow. Pain and hardship still come, but they are unable to drive out the happiness of the redeemed.

EUGENE PETERSON
A Long Obedience in the Same Direction

⋅ξ

From silly devotions and from sour-faced saints, good Lord, deliver us.

SAINT TERESA OF AVILA

❧

He who goes out weeping,
    carrying seed to sow,
will return with songs of joy,
    carrying sheaves with him.

Psalms 126:6

JUSTICE
❧

Justice without strength is helpless, strength without justice is tyrannical. . . . Unable to make what is just strong, we have made what is strong just.

BLAISE PASCAL

❧

It is justice, not charity, that is wanting in the world.

MARY WOLLSTONECRAFT

ঔঠ

How much easier it is to be generous than just! Men are sometimes bountiful who are not honest.

JUNIUS

ঔঠ

There's a wideness in God's mercy,
Like the wideness of the sea;
There's a kindness in His justice,
Which is more than liberty.

FREDERICK W. FABER

ঔঠ

For the Lord is a God of justice.
Blessed are all who wait for him!

Isaiah 30:18

KNOWLEDGE

Common sense is in spite of, not the result of, education.

VICTOR HUGO

He who has imagination without learning has wings but no feet.

JOSEPH JOUBERT

Virtue and learning, like gold, have their intrinsic value; but if they are not polished, they certainly lose a great deal of their lustre; and even polished brass will pass upon more people than rough gold.

LORD CHESTERFIELD

All perfection in this life hath some imperfection mixed with it; and no knowledge of ours is without some darkness.

THOMAS À KEMPIS

I would rather feel compunction in my heart than be able to define it.

THOMAS À KEMPIS

No man can survey himself without forthwith turning his thought towards the God in whom he lives and moves. . . . It is evident that man never attains to a true self-knowledge until he has previously contemplated the face of God and come down after such contemplation to look into himself.

JOHN CALVIN

A humble knowledge of thyself is a surer way to God than a deep search after learning.

THOMAS À KEMPIS

I often wonder if my knowledge about God has not become my greatest stumbling block to my knowledge of God.

HENRI NOUWEN
A Cry for Mercy

Grant me, O Lord, to know what is worth
    knowing,
to love what is worth loving,
to praise what delights you most,
to value what is precious in your sight,
to hate what is offensive to you.
Do not let me judge by what I see,
nor pass sentence according to what I hear,
but to judge rightly between things that
    differ,
and above all to search out and to do what
    pleases you,
through Jesus Christ our Lord.

THOMAS À KEMPIS

LONELINESS

My heart is a lonely hunter that hunts on a
lonely hill.

WILLIAM SHARP

We are born helpless. As soon as we are fully conscious we discover loneliness. We need others physically, emotionally, intellectually; we need them if we are to know anything, even ourselves.

C. S. LEWIS
The Four Loves

What loneliness is more lonely than distrust?

GEORGE ELIOT

Laugh and the world laughs with you;
  Weep, and you weep alone
For the sad old earth must borrow its mirth,
  But has trouble enough of its own.

ELLA WHEELER WILCOX

If the world seems cold to you,
  Kindle fires to warm it!

LUCY LARCOM

The important thing is to receive this moment's experience with both hands. Don't waste it.

ELISABETH ELLIOT
Passion and Purity

I will not leave you as orphans; I will come to you.

John 14:18

∽§

I will be with you always, to the very end of the age.

Matthew 28:20

∽§

In the strangling grip of Golgotha, our Savior experienced the maximum impact of loneliness. For an undisclosed period of time, the Father forsook Him. His friends had already fled. One had betrayed Him. Now the Father turned away. In the bottomless agony of that moment, our Lord cried—He literally screamed aloud. . . . Is it any wonder that He is now able to sympathize and enter in as we battle feelings of loneliness? Those who bear the scars of that silent warfare need no explanation of the pain—only an invitation to share in the wound and, if possible, help in the healing.

When we are lonely, we need an understanding friend. Jesus is the One who "sticks closer than a brother."

CHARLES SWINDOLL
Growing Strong in the Seasons of Life

LOVE

Love is patient, love is kind. It does not envy, it does not boast, it is not proud. It is not rude, it is not self-seeking, it is not easily angered, it keeps no record of wrongs. Love does not delight in evil but rejoices with the truth. It always protects, always trusts, always hopes, always perseveres.

1 Corinthians 13:4–7

One basic definition of love, as a verb, is "to value." Love should be a verb, not a noun or adverb. Love is an active emotion. It is not static. Love is one of the few experiences in life that we can best keep by giving it away. Love is the act of demonstrating value for and looking for the good in another person.

DENIS WAITLEY
Seeds of Greatness

The beloved John in his old age . . . was in the habit of saying little else to his disciples other than "little children, love one another." Eventually they became so fed up with always hearing the same thing that they asked him why he constantly repeated it. He replied, "Because it is the Lord's command and if it comes to pass, that suffices."

PHILIPP JACOB SPENER

Those who love not their fellow-beings, live unfruitful lives, and prepare for their old age a miserable grave.

PERCY BYSSHE SHELLEY

Love is ever the beginning of knowledge, as fire is of light.

THOMAS CARLYLE

They had souls large enough to feel the wrongs of others.

ELIZABETH CADY STANTON

I have generally found that those workers who are all the time looking to see how much they are going to get from the Lord are never satisfied. But love does its work and makes no bargain.

DWIGHT L. MOODY

A story is told of Jesus and His disciples walking one day along a stony road. Jesus asked each of them to choose a stone to carry for Him. John, it is said, chose a large one while Peter chose the smallest. Jesus led them then to the top of a mountain and commanded that the stones be made bread. Each disciple, by this time tired and hungry, was allowed to eat the bread he held in his hand, but of course Peter's was not sufficient to satisfy his hunger. John gave him some of his.

Some time later Jesus again asked the disciples to pick up a stone to carry. This time Peter chose the largest of all. Taking them to a river, Jesus told them to cast the stones into the water. They did so, but looked at one another in bewilderment.

"For whom," asked Jesus, "did you carry the stone?"

ELISABETH ELLIOT
These Strange Ashes

࿐

Dear children, let us not love with words or tongue but with actions and in truth.

1 John 3:18

LOVE OF GOD

Recently I was sent a picture of a jug into which water was being poured. The idea was that love, or whatever we need, is poured into us like that. I don't think of it so at all. I think of the love of God as a great river, pouring through us as the waters pour through our ravine in flood-time. Nothing can keep this love from pouring through us, except of course our own blocking of the river.

Do you sometimes feel that you have got to the end of your love for someone who refuses and repulses you? Such a thought is folly, for one cannot come to the end of what one has not got. We have no store of love at all. We are not jugs, we are river-beds.

AMY CARMICHAEL
Whispers of His Power

Oh, God, I did not know you were so big.

SOJOURNER TRUTH

God's gifts put man's best dreams to shame.

ELIZABETH BARRETT BROWNING

If you knew the whole Bible off by heart and all the expositions of scholars, what good would it do you without the love and grace of God.

THOMAS À KEMPIS

❧

Let us never forget that the love of God has moral depth and makes great demands. We sing silly little songs with titles such as "Somebody Up There Likes Me," and we talk about "The Man Upstairs," and we think of God's love as something that fits into a juke box. But God's love demands high living. When Jesus saw men of great promise giving themselves to fish nets, He said unto them, "Follow me, and I will make you fishers of men" (Matthew 4:19). Love calls to the highest life.

CHARLES L. ALLEN

❧

I have loved you with an everlasting love.

Jeremiah 31:3

MARRIAGE

Whoever lives true life, will love true love.

ELIZABETH BARRETT BROWNING

I . . . chose my wife as she did her wedding gown, not for a fine glossy surface, but such qualities as would wear well.

OLIVER GOLDSMITH

Keep your eyes wide open before marriage, half shut afterwards.

BENJAMIN FRANKLIN

Love is a glass which shatters if you hold it too tightly or too loosely.

Russian Proverb

Though familiarity may not breed contempt, it takes off the edge of admiration.

WILLIAM HAZLITT

. . . Love is not love
Which alters when it alteration finds,
Or bends with the remover to remove:
O, no! it is an ever-fixed mark,
That looks on tempests and is never shaken.

WILLIAM SHAKESPEARE

Marriage, like life itself, is both a giving and a taking away. What is given in marriage is fairly obvious: the love of another human being. What is taken away is perhaps not quite so apparent: the entire freedom to think and to act as an independent person.

MIKE MASON
The Mystery of Marriage

Two persons love in one another the future good which they aid one another to unfold.

MARGARET FULLER

People get from books the idea that if you have married the right person you may expect to go on "being in love" for ever. As a result, when they find they are not, they think this proves they have made a mistake and are entitled to a change—not realising that, when they have changed, the glamour will presently go out of the new love just as it went out of the old one. In this department of life, as in every other, thrills come at the beginning and do not last. . . .

Let the thrill go—let it die away—go on through that period of death into the quieter interest and happiness that follow—and you will find you are living in a world of new thrills all the time.

C. S. LEWIS
Mere Christianity

I like not only to be loved, but also to be told that I am loved.

GEORGE ELIOT

Grow old along with me!
The best is yet to be,
The last of life, for which the first was made:
Our times are in His hand
Who saith, "A whole I planned,
Youth shows but half. . . ."

ROBERT BROWNING

That I may come near to her, draw me nearer to thee than to her; that I may know her, make me to know thee more than her; that I may love her with the perfect love of a perfectly whole heart, cause me to love thee more than her and most of all. Amen. Amen.

That nothing may be between me and her, be thou between us, every moment. That we may be constantly together, draw us into separate loneliness with thyself. And when we meet breast to breast, my God, let it be on thine own. Amen. Amen.

TEMPLE GAIRDNER

MIRACLES

Miracles happen only to those who believe in them.

French Proverb

In all my life I have met only one person who claims to have seen a ghost. And the interesting thing about the story is that that person disbelieved in the immortal soul before she saw the ghost and still disbelieves after seeing it. She says that what she saw must have been an illusion or a trick of the nerves. And obviously she may be right. Seeing is not believing.

C. S. LEWIS
Miracles

&

"There's no use trying," she said: "one *can't* believe impossible things."

"I daresay you haven't had much practice," said the Queen. "When I was your age, I always did it for half-an-hour a day. Why, sometimes I've believed as many as six impossible things before breakfast."

LEWIS CARROLL

&

Whoso loves believes the impossible.

ELIZABETH BARRETT BROWNING

&

I have never seen a greater monster or miracle in
the world than myself.

MONTAIGNE

MONEY

Whoever loves money never has money enough;
whoever loves wealth is never satisfied with his
income.

Ecclesiastes 5:10

It is not the rich man only who is under the
dominion of things; they too are slaves who,
having no money, are unhappy from the lack of it.

GEORGE MACDONALD

If it be *things* that slay you, what matter whether things you have, or things you have not?

GEORGE MACDONALD

❧

Better a little with the fear of the Lord
    than great wealth with turmoil.
Better a meal of vegetables where there is love
    than a fattened calf with hatred.

Proverbs 15:16, 17

❧

Whatever you have, spend less.

SAMUEL JOHNSON

❧

Put not your trust in money, but put your money in trust.

OLIVER WENDELL HOLMES, SR.

❧

Our incomes are like our shoes; if too small, they gall and pinch us; but if too large, they cause us to stumble and to trip.

CHARLES CALEB COLTON

❧

Money *is* spiritual issue.

RICHARD FOSTER

Money, Sex and Power

For the Christian, the bottom line can never be the bottom line.

RICHARD FOSTER

Money, Sex and Power

MUSIC

The man that hath no music in himself,
Nor is not moved with concord of sweet
    sounds,
Is fit for treasons, stratagems, and spoils,
The motions of his spirit are dull as night,
And his affections dark as Erebus.
Let no such man be trusted. Mark the music.

WILLIAM SHAKESPEARE

Is it not strange that sheep's guts should hale souls out of men's bodies?

WILLIAM SHAKESPEARE

⊸§

It is extraordinary how music sends one back into memories of the past.

GEORGE SAND

⊸§

The music in my heart I bore
Long after it was heard no more.

WILLIAM WORDSWORTH

⊸§

By the rivers of Babylon we sat and wept
    when we remembered Zion.
There on the poplars
    we hung our harps,
for there our captors asked us for songs,
    our tormentors demanded songs of joy;
    they said, "Sing us one of the songs of
Zion!"
How can we sing the songs of the Lord
    while in a foreign land?

Psalms 137:1–4

⊸§

Who hears music, feels his solitude
Peopled at once.

ROBERT BROWNING

❧

And the night shall be filled with music
And the cares, that infest the day,
Shall fold their tents, like the Arabs,
And as silently steal away.

HENRY WADSWORTH LONGFELLOW

❧

If music be the food of love, play on.

WILLIAM SHAKESPEARE

❧

In My Heart There Rings a Melody.

ELTON M. ROTH

NATURE
❧

You are God. You want to make a forest,
something to hold the soil, lock up solar energy,

and give off oxygen. Wouldn't it be simpler just to rough in a slab of chemicals, a green acre of goo?

ANNIE DILLARD
Pilgrim at Tinker Creek

⁓§

Earth's crammed with heaven,
And every common bush afire with God;
But only he who sees takes off his shoes;
The rest sit round it and pluck blackberries.

ELIZABETH BARRETT BROWNING

⁓§

Men as a general rule have very little reverence for trees.

ELIZABETH CADY STANTON

⁓§

God writes the gospel not in the Bible alone, but on trees, and flowers, and clouds, and stars.

MARTIN LUTHER

⁓§

The sky is the daily bread of the eyes.

RALPH WALDO EMERSON

⁓§

All Nature ministers to Hope.

HARTLEY COLERIDGE

&

The birds I heard today, which, fortunately, did not come within the scope of my science, sang as freshly as if it had been the first morning of creation.

HENRY DAVID THOREAU

&

Beauty descends from God into nature: but there it would perish and does except when a Man appreciates it with worship and thus as it were *sends it back* to God so that through his consciousness what descended ascends again and the perfect circle is made.

C. S. LEWIS
They Stand Together

&

Then the Lord answered Job out of the storm.
He said: . . .
    Who fathers the drops of dew?
From whose womb comes the ice?

Who gives birth to the frost from the
heavens
when the waters become hard as stone,
    when the surface of the deep is frozen?
Can you bind the beautiful Pleiades?
    Can you loose the cords of Orion?
Can you bring forth the constellations in
their seasons
    or lead out the Bear with its cubs?
Do you know the laws of the heavens?
    Can you set up God's dominion over the
earth?

Job 38:1, 28–33

The heavens declare the glory of God;
    the skies proclaim the work of his hands.
Day after day they pour forth speech;
    night after night they display knowledge.

Psalms 19:1, 2

NEIGHBOR

A man must not choose his neighbour; he must take the neighbour that God sends him. . . . The neighbour is just the man who is next to you at the moment, the man with whom any business has brought you into contact.

GEORGE MACDONALD

"Who is my neighbor?"

In reply Jesus said: "A man was going down from Jerusalem to Jericho, when he fell into the hands of robbers. They stripped him of his clothes, beat him and went away, leaving him half dead. A priest happened to be going down the same road, and when he saw the man, he passed by on the other side. So too, a Levite, when he came to the place and saw him, passed by on the other side. But a Samaritan, as he traveled, came where the man was; and when he saw him, he took pity on him. He went to him and bandaged his wounds, pouring on oil and wine. Then he put the man on his own donkey, took him to an inn and took care of him. The next day he took out two silver coins and gave them to the innkeeper. 'Look after him.' he said, 'and when I return, I will reimburse you for any extra expense you may have.'

"Which of these three do you think was a neighbor to the man who fell into the hands of robbers?"

The expert in the law replied, "The one who had mercy on him."

Jesus told him, "Go and do likewise."

Luke 10:29–37

❧

We cannot be sure if we are loving God, although we may have good reasons for believing that we are, but we can know quite well if we are loving our neighbour.

SAINT TERESA OF AVILA

❧

Are you hypersensitive, suspicious, quarrelsome, wary, hostile, aggressive, contentious? You will never like your neighbor, because you don't like yourself. Are you quick-tempered, jealous, demanding, complaining? Same problem. If you want to associate on a good, friendly, normal, creative level with other people, you have to do a job on yourself—until you like yourself.

NORMAN VINCENT PEALE
Positive Imaging

❧

Love your neighbor as yourself.

Luke 10:27

❧

Love your neighbor, yet pull not down your hedge.

GEORGE HERBERT

❧

The love of our neighbour is the only door out of the dungeon of self, where we mope and mow, striking sparks, and rubbing phosphorescences out of the walls, and blowing our own breath in our own nostrils, instead of issuing to the fair sunlight of God, the sweet winds of the universe.

GEORGE MACDONALD

OBEDIENCE

❧

Rules, rules, rules. There are so many rules.

EVELYN BENCE

❧

Good manners are made up of petty sacrifices.

RALPH WALDO EMERSON

❧

Obedience, in its root meaning, is meant to communicate the notion of listening—more than just a haphazard listening, however. It indicates a straining to hear, a silent attentiveness that motivates our actions. A helpful image is one of two lovers in joyful embrace, straining to hear the other's sighs, rejoicing when words of love are spoken, and responding to the other's every request and movement. That is obedience.

CHRIS ARIDAS
Soundings

❧

Wicked men obey from fear; good men, from love.

ARISTOTLE

❧

"Take my life and let it be" is the impossible petition of a man or woman who wants the best of two worlds but who doesn't want to pay the list price for either.

KENNETH L. WILSON
All Things Considered

≈§

Instead of asking yourself whether you believe or not, ask yourself whether you have this day done one thing because He said, *Do it,* or once abstained because He said, *Do not do it.* It is simply absurd to say you believe, or even want to believe, in Him, if you do nothing He tells you.

GEORGE MACDONALD

≈§

We must obey God rather than men!

Acts 5:29

≈§

Obedience to God does not always mean a happy ending. But why should we think it would?

CHARLES COLSON
Loving God

≈§

"Putting out the fleece" hardly seems an appropriate model for someone seeking guidance: it better describes someone who knows exactly what God wants and still quakes before the task.

PHILIP YANCEY
Guidance

ᘓᔧ

To obey is better than sacrifice.

1 Samuel 15:22

OPPORTUNITY

ᘓᔧ

Ability is of little account without opportunity.

NAPOLEON BONAPARTE

ᘓᔧ

A wise man will make more opportunities than he finds.

FRANCIS BACON

ᘓᔧ

To improve the golden moment of opportunity, and catch the good that is within our reach, is the great art of life.

SAMUEL JOHNSON

The Chinese symbols for *crisis* are identical to those for the word *opportunity*. Literally translated it reads, "Crisis is an opportunity riding the dangerous wind."

DENIS WAITLEY
Seeds of Greatness

Work, for the night is coming,
When man's work is done.

ANNIE L. COGHILL

PAIN

Imagine a child saying to his parents, "I keep skinning my knees on the sidewalk! If you really loved me, you'd get that mean sidewalk out of here!" We don't remove the sidewalk; we help teach the child how to walk, roller skate, or ride the bike with skill and caution.

WARREN WIERSBE
Why Us?

How sickness enlarges the dimensions of a man's self to himself.

CHARLES LAMB

Pain—has an element of blank—
It cannot recollect
When it begun—or if there were
A time when it was not—

It has no future but—itself—
Its Infinite contain

Its Past—enlightened to perceive
New Periods—of—Pain.

EMILY DICKINSON

≈§

There are no graduates in the school of human
pain. . . . All too often we will be faced with the
necessity of relearning faith's lessons and of remak-
ing our commitments and renewing our vows.
Truths of Scripture that we thought we knew not
only by heart but by experience will have to be
reapplied to our souls to meet our daily need.

MARGARET CLARKSON
Grace Grows Best in Winter

≈§

Pain is no longer pain when it is past.

MARGARET PRESTON

≈§

Is there no balm in Gilead?
Is there no physician there?

Jeremiah 8:22

≈§

There is a balm in Gilead to make the wounded whole.

Spiritual

&

He forgives all my sins
   and heals all my diseases;
he redeems my life from the pit
   and crowns me with love and compassion.

Psalms 103:3, 4

&

Say the word, and my servant will be healed.

Luke 7:7

PATIENCE
&

He preaches patience that never knew pain.

HENRY GEORGE BOHN

&

Patience, hard thing! . . .
. . . Patience who asks
Wants war, wants wounds . . .

GERARD MANLEY HOPKINS

❧

The great believers have been the unwearied
waiters.

ANONYMOUS

❧

The principal part of faith is patience.

GEORGE MACDONALD

❧

Genius is only great patience.

GEORGE LOUIS LECLERC DE BUFFON

❧

I worked with patience, which means almost
power.

ELIZABETH BARRETT BROWNING

❧

Over the piano was printed a notice: Please do
not shoot the pianist. He is doing his best.

OSCAR WILDE

❧

Be patient, then, brothers, until the Lord's coming. See how the farmer waits for the land to yield its valuable crop and how patient he is for the fall and spring rains. You too, be patient and stand firm, because the Lord's coming is near.

James 5:7, 8

PEACE

I have told you these things, so that in me you may have peace. In the world you will have trouble. But take heart! I have overcome the world.

John 16:33

Like a river glorious
Is God's perfect peace,
Over all victorious
In its bright increase;
Perfect, yet it floweth

Fuller every day,
Perfect, yet it groweth
Deeper all the way.

FRANCES R. HAVERGAL

๛

Look unto Jesus. I looked on Jesus and the dove
of peace entered my heart. I looked at the dove of
peace; and lo . . . off he went.

CORRIE TEN BOOM
Each New Day

๛

Perhaps peace is not, after all, something you
work for, or "fight for." . . . Peace is something
you have or do not have. If you are yourself at
peace, then there is at least *some* peace in the world.
Then share your peace with everyone, and everyone
will be at peace.

THOMAS MERTON
Conjectures of a Guilty Bystander

๛

Lord, make me an instrument of your peace.
Where there is hatred, let me sow love,

Where there is injury, pardon,
Where there is doubt, faith,
Where there is despair, hope,
Where there is darkness, light,
Where there is sadness, joy.

SAINT FRANCIS OF ASSISI

Peace if possible, but truth at any rate.

MARTIN LUTHER

He who would be serene and pure needs but one
thing, detachment.

MEISTER ECKHART

Breathe through the heats of our desire
Thy coolness and Thy balm.
Let sense be dumb, let flesh retire;
Speak through the earthquake, wind, and
    fire,
O still small voice of calm!

Drop thy still dews of quietness,
Till all our strivings cease;

Take from our souls the strain and stress,
And let our ordered lives confess
The beauty of thy peace.

JOHN GREENLEAF WHITTIER

You will keep in perfect peace
him whose mind is steadfast,
because he trusts in you.

Isaiah 26:3

When you have laboriously accomplished your
daily task, go to sleep in peace. God is awake.

VICTOR HUGO

PERCEPTIONS

Beauty, we have all heard, is in the eye of the
beholder. When you're in love you may see beauty

that nobody else can see. When you think there's danger in your community, you may hear threatening sounds that nobody else hears. When you are seriously ill but hoping to recover, you may notice signs of improvement that the doctor doesn't see. A lot of life—how we think and act—depends on how we see the world.

GARY COLLINS
Getting Your Life Out of Neutral

The circumstances of others seem good to us, while ours seem good to others.

PUBLILIUS SYRUS

We are all apt to believe what the world believes about us.

GEORGE ELIOT

Self-contempt, bitterer to drink than blood.

PERCY BYSSHE SHELLEY

Beware of despairing about yourself: you are commanded to put your trust in God, and not in yourself.

SAINT AUGUSTINE

⋖§

Believe that life *is* worth living, and your belief will help create the fact.

WILLIAM JAMES

⋖§

Thomas Edison is well-known for his inventions such as the electric light bulb and the phonograph. Less well known, perhaps, is his tenacity in the face of what looked like failure. He tried five thousand different materials while seeking a filament that would make the electric light work. Did he see that as five thousand failures? No—instead, he called it "succeeding in learning five thousand different things that would not work!"

DENIS WAITLEY
The Double Win

⋖§

It is altogether the way we look at things whether we think they are crosses or not. I am ashamed to think that any Christian should ever put on a long face and shed tears over doing a thing for Christ which a worldly man would be only too glad to do for money or country.

HANNAH WHITALL SMITH

PERSEVERANCE

You have heard of Job's perseverance and have seen what the Lord finally brought about.

James 5:11

By perseverance the snail reached the ark.

CHARLES HADDON SPURGEON

Perseverance does not always mean sticking to the same thing forever. It means giving full concentration and effort to whatever you are doing, right now! It means doing the tough things first and looking downstream for gratification and rewards. . . . Perseverance is success through trial and error.

DENIS WAITLEY
Seeds of Greatness

Many a humble soul will be amazed to find that the seed it sowed in weakness, in the dust of daily life, has blossomed into immortal flowers under the eye of the Lord.

HARRIET BEECHER STOWE

Blot out, correct, insert, refine,
Enlarge, diminish, interline;
Be mindful, when invention fails,
To scratch your head, and bite your nails.

JONATHAN SWIFT

Little strokes,
Fell great oaks.

BENJAMIN FRANKLIN

Love . . . always perseveres.

> 1 Corinthians 13:6, 7

Well done, good and faithful servant! You have been faithful with a few things; I will put you in charge of many things.

> Matthew 25:23

POWER

I took my Power in my Hand—
And went against the World—
'Twas not so much as David—had—
But I—was twice as bold—

I aimed my Pebble—but Myself
Was all the one that fell—
Was it Goliah—was too large—
Or myself—too small?

EMILY DICKINSON

The three great apostles and supporters of practical atheism are Wealth, Health, and Power.

CHARLES CALEB COLTON

~§

It is a strange desire . . . to seek power over others, and to lose power over a man's self.

FRANCIS BACON

~§

You can't hold a man down without staying down with him.

BOOKER T. WASHINGTON

~§

No compromise is possible between our desire to dominate and the selfless service of Christian discipleship.

RICHARD HARRIES
Prayer and the Pursuit of Happiness

~§

There is a power that destroys. There is also a power that creates. The power that creates gives life and joy and peace. It is freedom and not bondage, life and not death, transformation and not coercion. The power that creates restores relationship and gives the gift of wholeness to all. The power that creates is spiritual power, the power that proceeds from God.

RICHARD FOSTER
Money, Sex and Power

It is Peter, weeping bitterly, who returns to greater power than ever.

VANCE HAVNER

For God did not give us a spirit of timidity, but a spirit of power, of love and of self-discipline.

2 Timothy 1:7

PRAYER

Prayer is the little implement
Through which Men reach

Where Presence—is denied them. . . .

EMILY DICKINSON

⋅⋗ξ

Prayer, in its simplest definition, is merely a wish turned God-ward.

PHILLIPS BROOKS

⋅⋗ξ

I throw myself down in my chamber, and I call in and invite God and his angels thither, and when they are there, I neglect God and his angels, for the noise of a fly, for the rattling of a coach, for the whining of a door.

JOHN DONNE

⋅⋗ξ

One way to recollect the mind easily in the time of prayer, and preserve it more in tranquillity, is not to let it wander too far at other times.

BROTHER LAWRENCE

⋅⋗ξ

My words fly up, my thoughts remain below:
Words without thoughts never to heaven go.

WILLIAM SHAKESPEARE

⋅⋗ξ

Those who always pray are necessary to those who never pray.

VICTOR HUGO

And why should the good of anyone depend on the prayer of another? I can only answer with the return question, "Why should my love be powerless to help another?"

GEORGE MACDONALD

It begins to seem as if the question of "answered prayers" is raised mainly by people who don't pray. It is as if they were saying, "What's in it for me? What can I get out of prayer?" This spirit is rather like that of certain bright students in college classes. They sit through the lecture trying to think of questions that will stump the professor. They are closing out the enlightenment they might receive by looking for a way to seize the role of authority figure for themselves. They are trying to second-guess God, to figure out how to get him to do it their way.

EMILIE GRIFFIN
Clinging

When you ask, you do not receive, because you ask with wrong motives, that you may spend what you get on your pleasures.

James 4:3

ᘓᶃ

And there is a communion with God that asks for nothing, yet asks for everything. . . . He who seeks the Father more than anything He can give, is likely to have what he asks, for he is not likely to ask amiss.

GEORGE MACDONALD

ᘓᶃ

Give us grace to listen well.

JOHN KEBLE

ᘓᶃ

Prayer is the most important thing in my life. If I should neglect prayer for a single day, I should lose a great deal of the fire of faith.

MARTIN LUTHER

ᘓᶃ

If you pray for bread and bring no basket to carry it, you prove the doubting spirit which may be the only hindrance to the boon you ask.

DWIGHT L. MOODY

ᘓᶃ

Pray continually.

1 Thessalonians 5:17

PRIDE

Proud people breed sad sorrows for themselves.

EMILY BRONTË

The tongue is a small part of the body, but it makes great boasts. Consider what a great forest is set on fire by a small spark. The tongue also is a fire.

James 3:5, 6

He was like a cock, who thought the sun had risen to hear him crow.

GEORGE ELIOT

The gifts of God are not given for ornament but for use. To strut like a peacock over your gifts is to view yourself in an ornamental mode only.

CALVIN MILLER
Becoming

A man is never so proud as when striking an attitude of humility.

C. S. LEWIS

I have had so many sincere Christians tell me that the ego of a Christian should be annihilated, so only Christ can live in its place. What an unhealthy pietism that is! A theology of worms, not men.

CALVIN MILLER
If This Be Love

God opposes the proud but gives grace to the humble.

1 Peter 5:5

O Lord,
never suffer us to think
that we can stand by ourselves,
and not need thee.

JOHN DONNE

REGRETS

In the life of each of us, I said to myself, there is a place remote and islanded, and given to endless regret or secret happiness.

SARAH ORNE JEWETT

Regret nothing. Not even the sins and failures. When a man views earth's wonders from some mountain height he does not spend his time in dwelling on the stones and stumbles, the faints and failures, that marked his upward path. . . .

For weal or woe each day is ended. What remains to be lived, the coming twenty-four hours, you must face as you awake.

TWO LISTENERS

God Calling

∽§

Trust no future, howe'er pleasant!
Let the dead past bury its dead!
Act,—act in the living Present!
Heart within and God o'erhead.

HENRY WADSWORTH LONGFELLOW

∽§

Regret not that which is past; and trust not to thine own righteousness.

SAINT ANTHONY

∽§

Reflect upon your present blessings, of which every man has many; not on your past misfortunes, of which all men have some.

CHARLES DICKENS

RESPONSIBILITY

Though we cannot by our own act lift ourselves out of the pit, we must by an act of our own take hold of the hand which offers to lift us out of it.

J. C. AND AUGUSTUS HARE

He who is false to present duty breaks a thread in the loom, and will find the flaw when he may have forgotten its cause.

HENRY WARD BEECHER

Duty is ours and events are God's.

JEANNE-FRANCOISE DEROIN

Starvation can take place because there is not any food—or because the food is not being eaten.

EDITH SCHAEFFER
A Way of Seeing

My spirit has become dry because it forgets to feed on you.

SAINT JOHN OF THE CROSS

If you leave a white post alone it will soon be a black post.

G. K. CHESTERTON

RESTLESSNESS

I have discovered that all human evil comes from this, man's being unable to sit still in a room.

BLAISE PASCAL

To be content with little is hard, to be content with much, impossible.

MARIE EBNER VON ESCHENBACH

I have learned the secret of being content in any and every situation, whether well fed or hungry, whether living in plenty or in want.

Philippians 4:12

It is not for man to rest in absolute contentment.

ROBERT SOUTHEY

❧

God knowingly placed us in an environment where there is always the possibility of sudden death. Why? . . . The only possible answer that is compatible with belief in a loving God is that (a) he has something more than finite security in mind for us, and (b) in order that we might be receptive to the possibility of receiving this ultimate security, it is necessary that we do not find everything we want in the created order.

RICHARD HARRIES
Prayer and the Pursuit of Happiness

❧

Thou hast made us for Thyself, and the heart of man is restless until it finds its rest in Thee.

SAINT AUGUSTINE

SECRETS

Three may keep a secret, if two of them are dead.

BENJAMIN FRANKLIN

Trust not him with secrets, who, when left alone in your room, turns over your papers.

JOHANN KASPAR LAVATER

The human heart has hidden treasures,
In secret kept, in silence sealed.

CHARLOTTE BRONTË

There's many a battle fought daily
The world knows nothing about.

PHOEBE CARY

When you give to the needy, do not let your left hand know what your right hand is doing, so that your giving may be in secret. Then your Father, who sees what is done in secret, will reward you.

Matthew 6:3, 4

God will judge men's secrets.

Romans 2:16

SELF-INTEREST

—❦—

Man seeks his own good at the whole world's cost.

ROBERT BROWNING

❦

The law of grab is the primal law of infancy.

ANTOINETTE BROWN BLACKWELL

❦

Hoarding is always based on greed. It is a me-first preoccupation that says, "I must get my share of the goods before the 'greedy people' do."

CALVIN MILLER
Becoming

❦

There is far more said in the Bible against covetousness than against either stealing or drunkenness.

DWIGHT L. MOODY

❧

The one principle of hell is—"I am my own!"

GEORGE MACDONALD

❧

One does not want to hear one's thoughts; most of them are not worth hearing.

MARGARET OLIPHANT

❧

That favorite subject, Myself.

JAMES BOSWELL

❧

I have been a selfish being all my life, in practice, though not in principle.

JANE AUSTEN

S E R V I C E

I am often, I believe, praying for others when I should be doing things for them. It's so much easier to pray for a bore than to go and see him.

C. S. LEWIS
Letters to Malcolm

Why stand we here trembling around
Calling on God for help, and not ourselves,
    in whom God dwells
Stretching a hand to save the falling Man?

WILLIAM BLAKE

It's people who must make the difference. Not a program.

JONI EARECKSON TADA
Choices ... Changes

The bee is more honored than other animals, not because she labors, but because she labors for others.

SAINT CHRYSOSTOM

The greatest thing a man can do for his heavenly
Father is to be kind to some of His other children.

HENRY DRUMMOND

❧

People may excite in themselves a glow of
compassion, not by toasting their feet at the fire
and saying, "Lord, teach me more compassion,"
but by going and seeking an object that requires
compassion.

HENRY WARD BEECHER

❧

For who is greater, the one who is at the table or
the one who serves?

Luke 22:27

❧

Thou art never weary, O Lord, of doing us good.
Let us never be weary of doing thee service.

JOHN WESLEY

❧

They also serve who only stand and wait.

JOHN MILTON

SIN

———————— ✌ ————————

We want perfection in other people, and yet we do not put right our own failings. . . . It is clear how rarely we apply to our neighbours the same standards as to ourselves.

THOMAS À KEMPIS

✌

How immense appear to us the sins that we have not committed.

MADAME NECKER

✌

That which we call sin in others is experiment for us.

RALPH WALDO EMERSON

✌

Evil is easy, and has infinite forms.

BLAISE PASCAL

✌

I knew a child who believed she had committed the sin against the Holy Ghost, because she had, in her toilette, made an improper use of a pin. Dare not to rebuke me for adducing the diseased fancy of a child in a weighty matter of theology. "Despise not one of these little ones." Would the theologians were as near the truth in such matters as the children. *Diseased fancy!* The child knew, *and was conscious that she knew,* that she was doing wrong because she had been forbidden. There was rational ground for her fear . . . He would not have told her she was silly, and "never to mind." Child as she was, might He not have said to her, "I do not condemn thee: go and sin no more"?

GEORGE MACDONALD

ᘓᢔ

Every sin is the result of a collaboration.

STEPHEN CRANE

ᘓᢔ

Sin is first a simple suggestion, then a strong imagination, then delight, then assent.

THOMAS À KEMPIS

ᘓᢔ

A hypocrite is a fellow who isn't himself on Sundays.

ANONYMOUS

ᘓᢔ

The recognition of sin is the beginning of salvation.

MARTIN LUTHER

ﻌ§

It is human to err; it is devilish to remain wilfully in error.

SAINT AUGUSTINE

ﻌ§

A curious thing happens to humans who tangle with skunks. Their nose hairs absorb the odor, so they sneak around trying to keep their distance from their friends because they think they stink. And indeed, to themselves, they do.

. . . The same thing occurs when we sin. Long after the noticeable consequences have passed from our lives, long after those around us have ceased to be offended by our reek, we live in the stench of our actions, for they have become a part of us. And like skunk, it takes more than tomato juice to restore us to an acceptable state.

JOHN LEAX
In Season and Out

ﻌ§

When we truly smell the stench of sin within us, it drives us helplessly and irresistibly to despair.

But God has provided a way for us to be freed from the evil within: it is through the door of repentance.

CHARLES COLSON
Loving God

No more let sins and sorrows grow,
Nor thorns infest the ground;
He comes to make His blessings flow
Far as the curse is found.

ISAAC WATTS

SOLITUDE

There is a fellowship more quiet even than solitude, and which, rightly understood, is solitude made perfect.

ROBERT LOUIS STEVENSON

Solitude may be heaven or hell, depending on how you use it. If it becomes the province of self-pity or depression, it will be a hell. But if it becomes a time of creating, it will become a point of celebration for yourself and others.

CALVIN MILLER
Becoming

❧

"God is the creative fire," one of my patients once wrote, "and the devil is the destructive fire!"

But just try to separate the destructive from the creative fire! It is all according to the use one makes of it. That same flame which is at the basis of the whole of civilization can, if we are not careful, start the most terrible conflagrations.

PAUL TOURNIER
The Person Reborn

❧

Solitude affects some people like wine; they must not take too much of it, for it flies to the head.

MARY COLERIDGE

❧

We live, in fact, in a world starved for solitude, silence, and privacy; and therefore starved for meditation and true friendship.

C. S. LEWIS
The Weight of Glory

⊰§

Remember how Saint Augustine tells us about his seeking God in many places and eventually finding Him within himself. . . . However quietly we speak, He is so near that He will hear us: we need no wings to go in search of Him but have only to find a place where we can be alone and look upon Him present within us.

SAINT TERESA OF AVILA

⊰§

The nurse of full-grown souls is solitude.

JAMES RUSSELL LOWELL

⊰§

The very best and utmost of attainment in this life is to remain still and let God act and speak in thee.

MEISTER ECKHART

⊰§

Solitude is as needful to the imagination as society is wholesome for the character.

JAMES RUSSELL LOWELL

⌇

Silence is the element in which great things fashion themselves together, that at length they may emerge, full-formed and majestic, into the daylight of Life, which they are henceforth to rule.

MAURICE MAETERLINCK

⌇

God is not solitary.

SAINT THOMAS AQUINAS

STRENGTH
⌇

In quietness and trust is your strength.

Isaiah 30:15

⌇

Nothing is so strong as gentleness: nothing so gentle as real strength.

SAINT FRANCIS DE SALES

⋙

The truest help we can render an afflicted man is not to take his burden from him, but to call out his best strength that he may be able to bear the burden.

PHILLIPS BROOKS

⋙

The joy of the Lord is your strength.

Nehemiah 8:10

⋙

Not to the strong is the battle,
not to the swift is the race;
but to the true and the faithful,
victory is promised through grace.

SALLIE MARTIN

⋙

The weakness of God is stronger than man's strength.

1 Corinthians 1:25

SUCCESS

Those who wish to succeed must ask the right preliminary questions.

ARISTOTLE

In order that people may be happy in their work, these three things are needed: They must be fit for it: They must not do too much of it: And they must have a sense of success in it.

JOHN RUSKIN

If you wish to succeed in life, make perseverance your bosom friend, experience your wise counselor, caution your elder brother, and hope your guardian genius.

JOSEPH ADDISON

It is success which disappoints us because we had so thoroughly expected it to be the crown of life.

EMILIE GRIFFIN
Turning

Nothing is so good as it seems beforehand.

GEORGE ELIOT

❧

Success is counted sweetest
By those who ne'er succeed. . . .

EMILY DICKINSON

❧

The fear of not succeeding is, for many people, the biggest obstacle in their way. It holds them back from trying anything at all. And for lack of trying they never give themselves a chance of succeeding—the very thing that would cure them of their doubts. It is not, after all, such a terrible thing not to succeed straight away in some new undertaking. What is serious is to give up, to become stuck in a life that just gets emptier.

PAUL TOURNIER
Learn to Grow Old

❧

Why should we be in such desperate haste to succeed, and in such desperate enterprises? If a man does not keep pace with his companions, perhaps it is because he hears a different drummer. Let him

step to the music which he hears, however mea-
sured or far away. It is not important that he
should mature as soon as an apple tree or an oak.
Shall he turn his spring into summer?

HENRY DAVID THOREAU

❧

Never count success by money gained. That is
not the mind of My Kingdom. Your success is the
measure of My Will and Mind that you have
revealed to those around you.

TWO LISTENERS
God Calling

TEMPTATION

❧

It is easier to stay out than get out.

MARK TWAIN

❧

Learn to say no; it will be of more use to you than to be able to read Latin.

CHARLES HADDON SPURGEON

᷍Ꭶ

It is easier to suppress the first desire than to satisfy all that follow it.

BENJAMIN FRANKLIN

᷍Ꭶ

I know all about the despair of overcoming chronic temptations. . . . *No amount* of falls will really undo us if we keep on picking ourselves up each time. We shall of course be very muddy and tattered children by the time we reach home. But the bathrooms are all ready, the towels put out, and the clean clothes in the airing cupboard. The only fatal thing is to lose one's temper and give it up. It is when we notice the dirt that God is most present in us; it is the very sign of His presence.

C. S. LEWIS
Letters of C. S. Lewis

᷍Ꭶ

And lead us not into temptation, but deliver us from the evil one.

Matthew 6:13

᷍Ꭶ

No temptation has seized you except what is common to man. And God is faithful; he will not let you be tempted beyond what you can bear. But when you are tempted, he will also provide a way out so that you can stand up under it.

1 Corinthians 10:13

TIME

There is a time to be born, and a time to die, says Solomon, and it is the memento of a truly wise man; but there is an interval between these two times of infinite importance.

LEIGH RICHMOND

Time is but the stream I go a-fishing in.

HENRY DAVID THOREAU

Dost thou love life? Then do not squander time; for that's the stuff life is made of.

BENJAMIN FRANKLIN

❧

Time is what we want most, but what alas! we use worst.

WILLIAM PENN

❧

We control the clock. . . . Although it always runs, we can use it as we choose. We can choose how long we work, how long we play, how long we rest, how long we worry, and how long we procrastinate.

DENIS WAITLEY
Seeds of Greatness

❧

There are no fragments so precious as those of time, and none are so heedlessly lost by people who cannot make a moment, and yet can waste years.

ROBERT MONTGOMERY

❧

For a thousand years in your sight
are like a day that has just gone by,
or like a watch in the night.

Psalms 90:4

～ॐ

Is is astonishing how short a time it takes for very wonderful things to happen.

FRANCES BURNETT

～ॐ

Wait for the wisest of all counselors, Time.

PERICLES

～ॐ

Time is the great physician.

BENJAMIN DISRAELI

～ॐ

I am the Alpha and the Omega, the Beginning and the End.

Revelation 21:6

～ॐ

Time, whose tooth gnaws away everything else, is powerless against truth.

THOMAS H. HUXLEY

TODAY

Every man's experience of to-day, is that he was a fool yesterday and the day before yesterday.— To-morrow he will most likely be of exactly the same opinion.

CHARLES MACKAY

This is the day the Lord has made;
let us rejoice and be glad in it.

Psalms 118:24

Who can tell what a day may bring forth?
Cause me therefore, gracious God,
to live every day as if it were to be my last,
for I know not but that it may be such.
Cause me to live now as I shall wish I had
    done
when I come to die.

THOMAS À KEMPIS

The great thing, if one can, is to stop regarding all the unpleasant things as interruptions of one's "own," or "real" life. The truth is of course that

what one calls the interruptions are precisely one's
real life—the life God is sending one day by day:
What one calls one's "real life" is a phantom of
one's own imagination.

C. S. LEWIS

They Stand Together

⪧

Instead of preaching the good news of the
Kingdom, He [Jesus] was forced to saw planks and
hammer nails. It was such menial work for the Son
of God to be doing. It caused Him to miss going
to college. Every day He held back, it seemed, was
a day lost. But the days went into months and into
years, and still He had to wait. His chance did not
come until He was thirty years old. In those days,
thirty years old was approaching old age.

But as you study His entire life, you begin to
feel that the waiting was part of God's plan.
Certainly Jesus used His circumstances in the finest
possible way. Instead of becoming bitter, instead
of surrendering His dreams, instead of turning to
some lesser purpose, He held fast to His promised
land and at the same time was faithful to life, day
by day. . . . The opportunities of His limited

"today" became the stones out of which He built His castle tomorrow.

CHARLES L. ALLEN

❧

Be useful where thou livest.

GEORGE HERBERT

❧

We look forward to the promise of each day, having discovered the secret that the good old days are here and now.

DENIS WAITLEY
Seeds of Greatness

❧

Lord, thou knowest how busy I must be this day.
If I forget thee, do not thou forget me.

SIR JACOB ASTLEY

❧

Lord, give us to go blithely on our business all this day, bring us to our resting beds weary and content and undishonoured, and grant us in the end the gift of sleep.

ROBERT LOUIS STEVENSON

❧

I tell you, now is the time of God's favor, now is the day of salvation.

2 Corinthians 6:2

This time, like all times, is a very good one if we but know what to do with it.

RALPH WALDO EMERSON

TRUST

Be courteous to all, but intimate with few; and let those few be well tried before you give them your confidence.

GEORGE WASHINGTON

Oh, the comfort, the inexpressible comfort of feeling safe with a person; having neither to weigh thoughts nor measure words, but to pour them all out, just as they are, chaff and grain together, knowing that a faithful hand will take and sift them, keep what is worth keeping, and then, with the breath of kindness, blow the rest away.

GEORGE ELIOT

❧

The glory of friendship is not the outstretched hand, nor the kindly smile nor the joy of companionship; it is the spirited inspiration that comes to one when he discovers that someone else believes in him and is willing to trust him.

RALPH WALDO EMERSON

❧

I would be true, for there are those who trust me.

HOWARD ARNOLD WALTER

❧

Now it is required that those who have been given a trust must prove faithful.

1 Corinthians 4:2

TRUTH

What! Shall I lie again to God? I have told him nothing but lies; and shall I speak again, and tell another lie to God?

SOJOURNER TRUTH

Truth has rough flavors if we bite it through.

GEORGE ELIOT

There is nothing so powerful as truth; and often nothing so strange.

DANIEL WEBSTER

A lie travels round the world while Truth is putting on her boots.

CHARLES HADDON SPURGEON

. . . oftentimes to win us to our harm
The instruments of darkness tell us truths,

Win us with honest trifles, to betray us
In deepest consequence.

WILLIAM SHAKESPEARE

⇜

The ultimate aim of the human mind, in all its
efforts, is to become acquainted with Truth.

ELIZA FARNHAM

⇜

It is not enough to possess a truth; it is essential
that the truth should possess us.

MAURICE MAETERLINCK

⇜

Jesus answered, "I am the way and the truth and
the life."

John 14:6

⇜

Then you will know the truth, and the truth
will set you free.

John 8:32

⇜

The greatest friend of truth is Time, her greatest
enemy is Prejudice, and her constant companion is
Humility.

CHARLES CALEB COLTON

❧

Doctrine is nothing but the skin of truth set up
and stuffed.

HENRY WARD BEECHER

❧

Love . . . rejoices with the Truth.

1 Corinthians 13:6

UNDERSTANDING
❧

Folks never understand the folks they hate.

JAMES RUSSELL LOWELL

❧

A man doesn't learn to understand anything unless he loves it.

JOHANN WOLFGANG VON GOETHE

≈§

Companions . . . endeavoured to show me "a more excellent way." But I understood it not at first. I was too learned and too wise. So that it seemed foolishness unto me.

JOHN WESLEY

≈§

He that will believe only what he can fully comprehend must have a very long head or a very short creed.

CHARLES CALEB COLTON

≈§

I do not understand; I pause; I examine.

MONTAIGNE

≈§

O Lord, help me not to despise or oppose what I do not understand.

WILLIAM PENN

WISDOM

I am sending you out like sheep among wolves. Therefore be as shrewd as snakes and as innocent as doves.

Matthew 10:16

Cleverness is not wisdom.

EURIPIDES

Knowledge comes, but wisdom lingers.

ALFRED, LORD TENNYSON

Inquire often, but judge rarely, and thou wilt not often be mistaken.

WILLIAM PENN

Be prudent, and if you hear . . . some insult or some threat . . . have the appearance of not hearing it.

GEORGE SAND

No man at one time can be wise and love.

ROBERT HERRICK

&

Some people hold . . . that there is a wisdom of the Head, and that there is a wisdom of the Heart.

CHARLES DICKENS

&

Wisdom never kicks at the iron walls it can't bring down.

OLIVE SCHREINER

&

If any of you lacks wisdom, he should ask God, who gives generously to all without finding fault, and it will be given to him. But when he asks, he must believe and not doubt, because he who doubts is like a wave of the sea, blown and tossed by the wind.

James 1:5, 6

&

Wisdom is proved right by all her children.

Luke 7:35

WITNESS

If a man cannot be a Christian in the place where he is, he cannot be a Christian anywhere.

HENRY WARD BEECHER

Could it be that we believers are the reason there are so many unbelievers?

KENNETH L. WILSON
All Things Considered

Kindness has converted more sinners than either zeal, eloquence, or learning.

FREDERICK W. FABER

I heard an old man, who seemed to overflow with joy and thanksgiving, say that his life had taken a turn when he committed himself to witness every day. By "witness" he did not mean an evangelistic appeal; he meant praising the Lord, "telling of his excellent greatness." He would not

let a day go by without telling *someone*—Christian
or non-Christian—of God's goodness.

TIM STAFFORD
Knowing the Face of God

๛

You will be my witnesses.

Acts 1:8

WORK

๛

Work consists of whatever a body is *obliged* to
do, and Play consists of whatever a body is not
obliged to do.

MARK TWAIN

๛

All work and no play makes Jack a dull boy.

JAMES HOWELL

๛

Sabbathless Satan.

CHARLES LAMB

⤳

A man is not idle because he is absorbed in thought. There is a visible labor and there is an invisible labor.

VICTOR HUGO

⤳

No race can prosper till it learns that there is as much dignity in tilling a field as in writing a poem.

BOOKER T. WASHINGTON

⤳

Here lies the body of John Smith, who for forty years cobbled shoes in this village to the glory of God.

Epitaph

⤳

I have been growing lately to feel that a great mistake of my past life . . . is an impatience of *results*. Inexperience of life is the cause of it, and I imagine it is an American characteristic. . . .

Results should not be too voluntarily aimed at or too busily thought of. They are *sure* to float up of their own accord, from a long enough daily work at a given matter; and I think the work as a mere occupation ought to be the primary interest with us.

WILLIAM JAMES

It is necessary for me to . . . apply myself industriously to whatever business I take in hand, and not divert my mind from my business by any foolish project of growing suddenly rich; for industry and patience are the surest means of plenty.

BENJAMIN FRANKLIN

Thunder is good, thunder is impressive; but it is lightning that does the work.

MARK TWAIN

Thank God every morning, when you get up, that you have something to do that day which must be done, whether you like it or not. Being forced to work, and forced to do your best, will breed in you

temperance and self-control, diligence and strength
of will, cheerfulness and content and a hundred
virtues which the idle man never knows.

CHARLES KINGSLEY

৺

He . . . must work, doing something useful
with his own hands, that he may have something
to share with those in need.

Ephesians 4:28

WORRY

৺

To carry care to bed is to sleep with a pack on
your back.

THOMAS CHANDLER HALIBURTON

৺

T'ain't worthwhile to wear a day all out before it
comes.

SARAH ORNE JEWETT

৺

Tomorrow makes today's whole head sick, its whole heart faint. When we should be still, sleeping or dreaming, we are fretting about an hour that lies a half sun's journey away.

GEORGE MACDONALD

❧

There are two things which are even more utterly incompatible than oil and water; trust and worry.

HANNAH WHITALL SMITH

❧

Do not fret because of evil men
   or be envious of those who do wrong;
for like the grass they will soon wither,
   like green plants they will soon die away.

Psalms 37:1, 2

❧

With every haunting trouble then, great or small, the loss of thousands or the lack of a shilling, go to God. . . . If your trouble is such that you cannot appeal to Him, the more need you should appeal to Him!

GEORGE MACDONALD

❧

Having laid my concern before the Father, I get
the feeling that if I do not frequently return to it in
my mind and keep "worrying" it, much as a dog
would a bone, then there certainly can be no chance
of solving it. It's a feeling that it would actually be
irresponsible or frivolous *not* to do this. . . .

I slip into the worry stance in spite of telling
myself over and over that God is the problem-
solver.

CATHERINE MARSHALL
A Closer Walk

⇜ঙ

Many persons distract themselves, first by their
fear of distraction, and then by their regret of such
distraction. What would you think of the traveller
who, instead of advancing on his way, was always
considering the accidents which he might meet
with and, after any accident, returned to contem-
plate the scene thereof? Would you not urge him
rather to go forward? Even so I say to you, Go on
without looking back, so that, pleasing God, you
may abound more and more.

FRANCOIS DE SALIGNAC DE LA MOTHE FENELON

⇜ঙ

The sovereign cure for worry is prayer.

WILLIAM JAMES

Do not be anxious about anything.

Philippians 4:6

WORSHIP

Wonder . . . is the basis of Worship.

THOMAS CARLYLE

If worship is to be a constant activity of the Christian . . . we must learn to juxtapose the seemingly unconnected. It's hard to understand how scrubbing the floor or taking the car to the garage for a tune-up has anything to do with worship, but somehow it does. The reason for worship may be different for each person; I would relate those activities to duty and responsibility and a lowly act of stewardship—caring for what God has given. Someone else might find a different reason to worship God for dirty floors or carburetors. Nothing in life is unimportant as a metaphor for imagination or worship. What is important is looking for them.

CHERYL FORBES
Imagination

❧

Do not forget that even as "to work is to worship" so to be cheery is to worship also, and to be happy is the first step to being pious.

ROBERT LOUIS STEVENSON

❧

God is to be worshipped by faith, hope, and love.

SAINT AUGUSTINE

❧

The goal of praise is not an experience; it is a relationship. The best aids to worship are those that because of their simplicity or familiarity

become clear as glass. We do not see them at all;
we see through them to the Lord.

TIM STAFFORD
Knowing the Face of God

≈§

God is spirit, and his worshipers must worship
in spirit and in truth.

John 4:24

≈§

Never wait for fitter time or place to talk to Him.
To wait till thou go to church or to thy closet is to
make Him wait. He will listen as thou walkest.

GEORGE MACDONALD

YOUTH
≈§

I felt so young, so strong, so sure of God.

ELIZABETH BARRETT BROWNING

≈§

The thoughts of youth are long, long thoughts.

HENRY WADSWORTH LONGFELLOW

Calm's not life's crown, though calm is well,
'Tis all perhaps which man acquires,
But 'tis not what our youth desires.

MATTHEW ARNOLD

When we are young we think things will go on
just as they are for ever. But they don't.

AMY CARMICHAEL
Whispers of His Power

We don't believe in rheumatism and true love
until after the first attack.

MARIE EBNER VON ESCHENBACH

Youth is wholly experimental.

ROBERT LOUIS STEVENSON

One wastes so much time, one is so prodigal of
life at twenty!

GEORGE SAND

Youth is like spring, an overpraised season.

SAMUEL BUTLER

એ

Give me the young man who has brains enough
to make a fool of himself!

ROBERT LOUIS STEVENSON

એ

Remember your Creator in the days of your
youth.

Ecclesiastes 12:1

THE LAST WORDS

The end of a matter is better than its beginning.

Ecclesiastes 7:8

God bless us every one.

CHARLES DICKENS

SOURCE INDEX

SCRIPTURE INDEX